Jonathan Holmes

Int

Methuen Drama

Published by Methuen Drama 2011

Methuen Drama, an imprint of Bloomsbury Publishing Plc

1 3 5 7 9 10 8 6 4 2

Methuen Drama
Bloomsbury Publishing Plc
36 Soho Square
London W1D 3QY
www.methuendrama.com

First published by Methuen Drama in 2011

ISBN: 978 1 408 15652 0

A CIP catalogue record for this book is available from the British Library

Available in the USA from Bloomsbury Academic & Professional, 175 Fifth
Avenue/3rd Floor, New York, NY 10010. www.BloomsburyAcademicUSA.com

Typeset by Mark Heslington Ltd, Scarborough, North Yorkshire
Printed and bound in Great Britain by CPI Antony Rowe, Chippenham
and Eastbourne

Jericho House

presents

Into Thy Hands

by Jonathan Holmes

First presented at Wilton's Music Hall on 2 June 2011
Produced by Jericho House and Wilton's Music Hall

Into Thy Hands

By Jonathan Holmes

Produced by Jericho House and Wilton's Music Hall

Cast

John Donne	Zubin Varla
Ann Donne	Jess Murphy
Lucy, Countess of Bedford	Stephanie Langton
Lancelot Andrewes	Nicholas Rowe
Lady Magdalene Danvers	Helen Masters
John Layfield/Alfonso Ferrabosco	Stephen Fewell
Sir Henry Wotton/King James I	Bob Cryer
Esther/courtier/dancer	Lorna Nickson-Brown/Sophie Ward
Musician/attendant	Emily Baines

Crew

Director	Jonathan Holmes
Producers	Jasmine Pajdak
	Jonathan Holmes
Assistant Producer	Kate Schofield
Set & Costume Designer	Lucy Wilkinson
Lighting Designer/Technical Manager	Filippo de Capitani
Company/Deputy Stage Manager	Suzie Foster
Musical Director	Emily Baines
Press	Anwen Hooson, Liz Hyder
	(for Riot Communications)
Assistant Designer	Kate Matthews
Design Assistants	Rachel Quinn
	Ottilie Purcell
ASM/Carpenter(rehearsals)	Ben Austin
ASM/Wardrobe (production)	Lorna Nickson-Brown/Sophie Ward
Scenic Painter	Elizabeth Vicary
Poster & Leaflet Image	Lucy Wilkinson
Box Office	Jane Thomas & the team at the
	Barbican Box Office

Music: 'Sweet Stay Awhile' (music: John Dowland, lyric: John Donne)
'Hymn to God the Father' (music: John Wilson, lyric: John Donne)
'Break of Day' (music: Orlando Gibbons, lyric: John Donne)
Music from 'Love Freed from Ignorance and Folly' by Alfonso
Ferrabosco and Robert Johnson.

Acknowledgements

The producers wish to thank the following, for all their help in enabling *Into Thy Hands* to happen:

Funders

David Lloyd, License My Roving Hands, John Garrett, John B. Birchell Hughes, Rt Rev Harries, Baroness Campbell of Surbiton.

Supporters

Leonora Wood, Suzanne Cristinacce, Peter Readman, Nick Price, Company XIV, Guildhall School of Music and Drama, Tom Mclaughlin, Kirsten Mclaughlin, Vanessa Garrett, Romany Pajdak, Jurek Pajdak, Lauren Witts, Rosa Sutcliff, Piera Buckland, Tom Goodman-Hill, Orlando Wells, Shereen Martineau, Orla Brady, Naomi Trickey, Harriet Walter, Elliot Cowan, Michael Vale, Sonia Fraser, Daniel Evans, Jamie Archer, Charlotte Loveridge, Matthew Byam-Shaw, Nicola Wass, Tobias Round, Kate de Rycker, Christopher Simpson, Emma Kirkby, Janet Suzman, Dolja Gavanski, Josephine D'Arby, Lucy Mclaughlin, Peter Case, Colin Denis and the London Fire Brigade (Whitechapel branch), Sally Miller at Tower Hamlets, Leanne Cosby, Moira Yip, Bridget O'Brien-Twohig, Louise Jeffreys, Keith Steadman.

Fundraising for such a large production could not have been achieved without the help of a number of dedicated artists and volunteers who gave their time and their talent so generously at our performance of the masque 'Love Freed from Ignorance and Folly' in March 2011, in particular the dancers from the Royal Ballet. We wish to thank them all for their generous support and time.

A very special thanks must be reserved for David Lloyd, a remarkable friend without whom this production would never have been possible.

Jericho House tells unusual stories in unconventional spaces.

Brilliant cutting edge theatre. An exceptional audience experience. – *Jon Snow*

Not to be missed, immensely powerful. – *Alan Rickman*

Intense and important work. Groundbreaking stuff. – *Joanna Lumley*

Our previous work has included:

Fallujah (with the ICA, on Brick Lane, 2007). A found-space, testimony play about the sieges of that city in 2003 and 2005. It remains the only multi-dimensional account of the greatest military atrocity of the Iraq War, and led to revelations about chemical weapons usage on civilian populations. Cast included: Harriet Walter, Imogen Stubbs, Irene Jacob, Chipo Chung, Christopher Simpson, Shereen Martineau, Chris Jarman, Dominic Jephcott. Music: Nitin Sawhney. Set: Lucy Orta.

A rare and valuable bulletin from the butchery. – **Time Out**

Informative, courageous, and a moral tonic for the conscience. – **Sunday Times**

A devastating new piece of documentary theatre. – **Daily Telegraph**

Katrina (with the Young Vic, Bargehouse, 2009). A promenade, testimony play about the aftermath of the hurricane in New Orleans. It featured re-creations of real New Orleans houses and bars, and a score made of local music. Cast included: Andrea Harris, Wunmi Mosaku, Joe Speare, Andrew Dennis, Stephanie Langton, Orlando Wells. Music: Peter Readman and Michael Mwenso. Design: Lucy Wilkinson.

As riveting an example of site-specific theatre as I've seen. – **The Times** *(Benedict Nightingale) – also Critics' Choice*

Jonathan Holmes's uplifting, moving, promenade piece should blow you away . . . It protests, educates, asks for empathy and does this outstandingly well exposing the failure of the US government to cope with the crisis. – **Observer** *(Kate Kellaway)*

The stories build up a staggering picture of official lies and personal heroism. – **Guardian** *(Michael Billington)*

[The production] . . . has a heart-stopping directness. – **Daily Telegraph**

What's the point of art?

Jericho also runs an ongoing series of talks entitled *'What's the point of art?'*

Speakers have so far included: Brian Eno, Armando Iannucci, Karen Armstrong, A.L. Kennedy, Ziauddin Sardar, Siobhan Davies, Susie Orbach, Philippe Sands, Kwame Kwei-Armah, Henry March, David Puttnam and Chris Smith.

Perpetual Peace

In 2010 our first feature film, **Perpetual Peace,** premiered at the South African International Film Festival. It documents grassroots peacemaking strategies in conflict zones around the world, and features contributions from Jeremy Greenstock, George Monbiot, John Berger, Noreena Hertz, Karen Armstrong, Harold Pinter and many more.

Future work – *The Tempest*

Our next project is a 400th anniversary production of **The Tempest** for the Barbican's BITE 2011 season. **The Tempest** will tour Palestine and Israel in September 2011 before returning to London, where it will play offsite for five weeks at the church of St Giles, within the Barbican complex.

Company:
Artistic Director – Jonathan Holmes
Company Administrator – Suzanne Cristinacce
Associate Designer – Lucy Wilkinson
Associate Composer – Peter Readman
Website – Nick Price

Trustees: David Altaras, Polly McLean (chair), Holly Jamieson, Martin Trickey
Patron: Roger Graef, OBE

Press: RIOT Communications. Contact: anwen@riotcommunications.com

Jericho does not receive any support from the Arts Council. We would therefore like to thank all our generous supporters and friends, past and present, for enabling us to make the work we do. In a very real sense, we could not continue without you.

If you want to find out more about us, or get involved, we'd love to hear from you:

Contact: Suzanne@jerichohouse.org.uk.

info@jerichohouse.org.uk
www.jerichohouse.org.uk

WILTON'S

THE CITY'S HIDDEN STAGE

Wilton's is the world's oldest surviving grand music hall and London's best kept secret. This stunning and atmospheric building is home to an exciting programme of diverse and distinct entertainment including theatre, music, comedy, cinema and cabaret.

The hall has a colourful and rich history. It was built in 1858 by John Wilton who had the vision to create a grand music hall. It was a success from the start and some of the greatest music hall stars performed here, such as Champagne Charlie and Arthur Lloyd. Some historians even argue that Britain's first Can Can was seen on Wilton's stage!

By the 1880s new fire regulations marked the demise of its use and the hall closed. It was then purchased by a local Wesleyan Mission and used until the 1950s as a Methodist Mission, witnessing major moments in history such as the Dockers' Strike of 1889, the Battle of Cable Street in 1936 and two World Wars. When the Methodists left, Wilton's became derelict, unstable and under threat.

The building's fortunes have now changed and over the past few years it has been lovingly and sensitively brought to life by the Wilton's Music Hall Trust. A capital project is under way to conserve and protect the structure and fabric the building, while the team continue to produce an imaginative array of live events that celebrate its past yet define a vibrant future.

Artistic Director	Frances Mayhew
Development Director	Kate Mitchell
Technical Manager	Filippo de Capitani
Building Manager	Jon Freeman
Marketing Manager	Oona Patterson
Administrator	Becky Ruffell
Theatre Technician	John Quigley
Researcher and Tour Guide	Carole Zeidman
Friends Volunteer	Stephanie Riley
Financial Advisor	Barry Sutcliffe

The Mahogany Bar Team: Dennis Pascual, Flaminia De Martino, Nick Horton, Rachel Richardson, Emma Edwards, Philip Meehan

Associate Artists: Peter Sheppard-Skaerved, Peter Case, Katherine Rhodes, Netia Jones, Nicky Gayner, Noel Wallace

WILTON'S

THE CITY'S HIDDEN STAGE

Help Support Wilton's

Wilton's, the world's oldest grand music hall, is a charity and receives no public funding. It uses an entrepreneurial spirit to survive and generates income from location hire, box office revenue and bar sales. Wilton's, however, still needs to generate additional income to keep this vibrant cultural venue alive. Please help us do this by joining Wilton's Friends or Patrons Scheme, email mailing list, or by coming for a drink at the Mahogany Bar. More information is available from the box office, at www.wiltons.org.uk or by calling 020 7702 9555.

Current Supporters

We would like to thank our generous supporters listed below as well as all of our Friends and volunteers.

Individuals

Anonymous
Mr and Mrs Sherban Cantacuzino
Clyde Cooper
Fredo Donnelly and Mike Richardson
Ruth Finch
Andrew Gorman
Mr and Mrs Nicholas Harris
George Law

Henry Lewis
Mark and Liza Loveday
Joan Major
David and Jane Pennock
John and Stephanie Riley
Reverend David Rogers
Jan and Michael Topham
Eddy Smith

Corporates

Carlsberg
Cluttons
The Corner Shop PR
Latham and Watkins LLP
N1 Creative

Radisson Edwardian – Official Hotel Sponsor
Times+
Astell Scientific

Trusts and Foundations

The National Trust
The Noël Coward Foundation
The Foundation for Sport and the Arts
The Anthony Hornby Trust
The Stuart and Hilary Williams Charitable Foundation

The National Trust
The Noël Coward Foundation
The Foundation for Sport and the Arts
The Anthony Hornby Trust
The Stuart and Hilary Williams Charitable Foundation

WILTON'S MUSIC HALL. GRACES ALLEY, LONDON E1 8JB,
TEL: 020 7702 9555, WEB: WWW.WILTONS.ORG.UK
REGISTERED CHARITY NO.1003041

Biographies

Filippo de Capitani – Lighting Designer/Production Manager

Filippo de Capitani is the technical manager at Wilton's, and he has lit and designed most of the shows at Wilton's in the last two years. Previously he was resident at LaMama ETC of New York and at the Berliner Ensemble in Berlin. His work has been presented in more than 400 theatres around the world, including Zurich Opera House, Le Palais des Glaces Paris, Piccolo Teatro Milan, Arsenale of Venice, Raffles Hotel Singapore, National Theatre Kyoto, National Theatre Taiwan, Actors Studio Kuala Lampur, Stadt Theatre of Dortmund and Frankfurt, Patravadi Theatre Bangkok and Akademie der Kunste Berlin. He has worked with directors such as Ellen Stewart, Bob Wilson, Andrei Serban, Yoshi Oida, Tom O'Horgan and Deborah Warner. He would love to thank Ellen Stewart.

Bob Cryer – Lord Henry Wotton/King James I

Bob studied English & Theatre at Warwick University and Classical Acting at LAMDA.

Theatre: includes Orsino in *Twelfth Night* (Theatre Royal Plymouth & tour), Elvis in Steve Martin's *Picasso at the Lapin Agile* (West Yorkshire Playhouse – European premiere), Bracciano in *The White Devil* (Brighton Dome), Coriolanus in *Coriolanus* (Edinburgh Fringe), Neal in *Love & Understanding* and Judas Iscariot in *Guerilla/Whore* (both Tabard Theatre).

Television: includes *EastEnders*, *Holby City*, *Coronation Street*, *The Bill*, *Our Hidden Lives*, *Crown Heights*, *Jake 2.0*, *Victoria Wood's Christmas Special*.

Stephen Fewell – John Layfield/Alfonso Ferrabosco

Stephen studied at Oxford University and trained at the Webber Douglas Academy.

Theatre: includes Arthur Andersen in the Olivier Award-winning *ENRON* (Chichester, Royal Court and West End), *Billy Bow* (Nuffield), Gabriel and Death in Headlong's *Paradise Lost*, *Henry IV Parts I & II* (Bristol Old Vic), Christopher Marlowe in *The Lie*, *The Tempest* (King's Head), *Only When I Laugh*, *Under the Yum-Yum Tree* (Mill, Sonning), *Macbeth*, *Romeo and Juliet* (Salisbury Playhouse & tour) *Lady Windermere's Fan* (Manchester Royal Exchange & tour), *Twelfth Night* (BAC), *The Long and the Short and the Tall* (West End), *The Metamorphoses* (Clod Ensemble), *Travels with My Aunt* (Leicester Haymarket & tour), *Beauty and the Beast* (Coventry Belgrade), *Of Thee I Sing* (Barbican).

Television and film: includes *The Courtroom* (Channel 4), *All Rise for Julian Clary* (BBC), *Sexdrive* (Independent).

Radio: includes Jason Kane in Big Finish's Bernice Summerfield series, *Doctor Who* (BBC7).

Stephen is currently chair of the JMK Trust for young theatre directors and is the author of several published short stories.

Suzie Foster – Company/Deputy Stage Manager

Jersey-born, Suzie trained at Jersey Arts Centre and Bristol University. Her theatre credits include the Edinburgh Fringe (Rich Hall's *Levelland*, *The Odd Couple*, *12 Angry Men* and the critically acclaimed *Charlie Victor Romeo*), the West End (*One Flew Over the Cuckoo's Nest)* and work with Guy Masterson Productions, little wonder, Watershed Productions and Central School of Speech and Drama. She has toured with Jersey Arts Centre, SCAMP and Fresh Glory Productions, both nationally and to Germany, Corfu, Dubai, Australia and New Zealand. Suzie was nominated for the Stage Management Association Individual Award in 2006. She also works for the London-based children's charity Scene & Heard.

www.suziefoster.com

Jonathan Holmes – Writer/Director

Jonathan Holmes is the director and founder of Jericho House. In 2007 he wrote and directed the testimony play *Fallujah*. In 2008 with The Sixteen he revived Henze and Bond's opera *Orpheus Behind the Wire* at the South Bank Centre, and in 2009 his testimony play *Katrina*, about New Orleans and produced in association with the Young Vic, sold out for a month in a warehouse in Southwark. In 2010 his documentary feature film *Perpetual Peace* was premiered at the South Africa International Film Festival. It followed previous documentary shorts made in Uganda, Kenya, Argentina and Antarctica. He also wrote the libretto for the 2011 opera *The Tongue of the Invisible* by Liza Lim (based on the poetry of Hafez), which premiered in Amsterdam and Koln, and was consultant on Freedom Studios' site-specific project *The Mill*, in Bradford. In Autumn 2011 his production of *The Tempest* will tour Palestine/Israel before returning for a five-week run at the Barbican.

He has a PhD from The Shakespeare Institute and for six years he taught Drama and English at Royal Holloway, University of London. Whilst there he published many articles and two books on Renaissance poetics. In 2005 he recovered and premiered several songs by John Donne at St Paul's Cathedral, where they were performed by Dame Emma Kirkby, The Sixteen and Carolyn Sampson. He has also written for a variety of periodicals and newspapers, including *Modern Poetry in Translation*, *Shakespeare Survey*, *Guardian*, *Independent* and *The Times*.

Stephanie Langton – Lucy Russell, Countess of Bedford

Stephanie trained at Drama Studio London.

Theatre: includes *Katrina* (Jericho House), Aaron Sorkin's *A Few Good Men* (Theatre Royal Haymarket), Sir Richard Eyre's *Hedda Gabler* (Duke of York's), *The Things Good Men Do* (Lyric Hammersmith), *Fool for Love, Closer, Comedy of Errors, The Country* (Belgrade Theatre, Coventry).

Film: includes Hong Kong/UK action movie *Bodyguard: A New Beginning.*

Television: includes *Law & Order UK* (BBC), *Holby Blue* (BBC), *Murdoch Mysteries* (CityTV, Alibi), *Werewolves* (Discovery/ITV Global), the BAFTA-winning *The Government Inspector* (Channel 4), *Jekyll* (BBC).

Helen Masters – Lady Magdalene Danvers

Helen trained at Webber Douglas Academy of Dramatic Art.

Theatre: includes *Betrayal* (Chester Gateway Theatre), *Acid Hearts* (Finborough Arms Theatre), *The Traveller* (Leicester Haymarket/Almeida), *Marya* (Old Vic), *The Country Wife* (Mermaid Theatre), *Les Liaisons Dangereuses* (Ambassadors, West End), *East, A Clockwork Orange* (Edinburgh Festival).

Television: includes *Doctors, Midsomer Murders, Web of Belonging* (Channel 4 film), *Holby City, A Touch of Frost, The Savages, Wycliffe* (Series 1 to 5 and Christmas Special) *The Paul Merton Show, Drop the Dead Donkey, Minder, Made in Heaven, Diana: Her True Story* (NBC film), *A Wreath of Roses* (ITV film).

Film: *The Affair of the Necklace.*

Jess Murphy – Ann Donne

Jess trained at Drama Studio London.

Theatre: includes *Blood Wedding* (Almeida), *Playing for Time* (Salisbury Playhouse), *Amadeus* (Wilton's Music Hall), *Brief Encounter* (Kneehigh), *Bedroom Farce* (the little theatre), *The Unspeakable* (English Touring Theatre), *The Hostage* (Southwark Playhouse), *War Horse* (National Theatre/West End).

Film: includes *Hereafter* (Warner Bros), *A Weekend in Venice* (Channel 4), *Sweeney Todd* (Warner Bros).

Jasmine Pajdak – Producer

Jasmine Pajdak holds a first class honours degree in Fine Art from University College Falmouth, where she specialised in mixed media (2009). In 2009 she was awarded the Barns-Graham Travel to Italy Scholarship. Jasmine has since completed a foundation film course at London Film Academy and worked for several London art galleries. Since joining the Jericho House team in December 2009 she has been fundraising for the new production, *Into Thy Hands*. In 2010 she initiated the non-profit project 'License My Roving Hands' to bring together different art disciplines to support, champion and fund creative endeavour – art working for art's sake. In collaboration with Wilton's Music Hall in 2011 she co-produced and co-ordinated the Jericho House's Jacobean masque 'Love Freed from Ignorance and Folly', and was instrumental in engaging the services of dancers from the Royal Ballet and from the American dance-theatre troupe Company XIV.

Nicholas Rowe – Lancelot Andrewes

Nicholas trained at Bristol Old Vic Theatre School.

Theatre: includes *Nation* (National Theatre), *Victory* (Arcola), *An English Tragedy*, (Palace Theatre Watford), *Whipping It Up*, (Bush Theatre and New Ambassadors), *See How They Run* (Duchess), *Rosencrantz and Guildenstern are Dead* (English Touring Theatre), *The Way of the World* (Wilton's Music Hall), *The Importance of Being Earnest* (Nottingham Playhouse), *Twelfth Night* (Sheffield Theatre), *Translations* (Royal Lyceum, Edinburgh), *Black Comedy/The Real Inspector Hound* (Donmar/Comedy Theatre), *Hamlet* (Hackney Empire and Broadway), *Saint Joan* (Theatre Clywd and West End), *The Fairy Queen* (Lisbon Coliseum), *Romeo and Juliet* (E.S.C), *My Cousin Rachel* (Derby Playhouse and Cheltenham Everyman).

Film: includes *The Duel* (Duel/Mainframe Productions), *The Baker* (Picture Farm), *Nicholas Nickleby* (United Artists), *Enigma* (Codebreaker Productions), *All Forgotten* (Steve Hills Pictures), *Lock, Stock and Two Smoking Barrels* (SKA Films), *True Blue* (Channel Four Films), *Young Sherlock Holmes* (Paramount), *Another Country* (Goldcrest).

Television: includes *Borgias* (Showtime), *Kingdom* (Kingdom Productions for ITV), *Margaret* (Great Meadow Productions), *Hotel Babylon* (Carnival), *Sold* (Touchpaper), *Beau Brummel* (Flashback), *Harlot's Progress* (Hartswood Films for Channel 4), *Gil Mayo* (BBC), *Waste of Shame* (BBC), *Our Hidden Lives* (BBC), *Broken News* (BBC), *Princes in the Tower* (RDF Media for Channel 4), *The Fugitives* (Shed Productions), *The Black Death* (Granada), *Midsomer Murders* (Bentley Productions), *La Femme Musketeer* (Hallmark), *Shackleton* (Firstsight Films Ltd), *Outside the Rules* (BBC), *Longitude* (Granada), *A Dance to the Music of Time* (Channel 4), *The Relic Hunters* (Gaumont Television), *Let Them Eat Cake* (Tiger Aspect), *Magpie in the Dock* (BBC), *The Prodigious Hickey* (Barharbour Films), *Sharpe's Enemy* (Central), *Poldark* (HTV), *Dalziel and Pascoe* (BBC), *Kavanagh QC* (Carlton).

Zubin Varla – John Donne

Zubin trained at the Guildhall School of Music and Drama.

Theatre: includes *War Horse* (National Theatre/New London Theatre), *Twelfth Night* (Donmar, West End), *Paradise Regained* (Royal Court), *The Enchantment, Attempts on Her Life, The Life of Galileo, Cyrano de Bergerac* (NT), *Julius Caesar* (Lyric, Hammersmith), *Julius Caesar, Two Gentlemen of Verona, Midnight's Children, The Tempest, Roberto Zucco, Bartholomew Fair, Faust, The Painter of Dishonour, Romeo and Juliet* (RSC), *Antigone* (Warehouse Production, Old Vic), *Jesus Christ Superstar* (Lyceum), *Amadeus* (City of London Sinfonia & UK tour), *Hello and Goodbye* (Southwark Playhouse), *Teeth 'n' Smiles* (Sheffield Crucible), *Chess* (Danish tour), *In the Solitude of Cotton Fields* (ATC), *A Day Like Today* (Young Vic), *Beautiful Thing* (Duke of York's), *In the Heart of America* (Bush), *A Connecticut Yankee in the Court of King Arthur, Romeo and Juliet, Lady Be Good* (Regent's Park Open Air).

Film and television: includes *Mad, Sad & Bad, Jacob, Hustle, Little Dorrit, Saddam's Tribe, Silent Witness, Spooks, Twelfth Night, Dalziel and Pascoe, Crocodile Shoes, Luv.*

Radio: includes *The Changeling, The Threepenny Opera, The Prospect II, ID, The Inheritance of Loss, A Dish of Pomegranates, The Wizard of Oz, Season of Migration to the North, Gandhi's Goat, The Night of the Mi'Rag, The Mahabharata.*

Lucy Wilkinson – Designer

Lucy Wilkinson, MA Illustration/Animation (Manchester School of Art), English Literature (Oxford University), Postgrad Dip Theatre Design (Bristol Old Vic Theatre School). Shortlisted for the 2005 Linbury Prize for Stage Design and the Jocelyn Herbert Award for Stage Design. Lucy is now Associate Designer with Jericho House.

Design credits: *The Tempest* (Barbican, to come) *Into Thy Hands, Love Freed: A Masque, Katrina, Fallujah* (Jericho), *Frozen,* Fresh Glory (Riverside Studios), *Company, Chook Chook* (Bristol Old Vic), *The Marriage of Figaro* (Redgrave, Bristol), *The Marriage of Figaro* (Warwick Arts), *Iolanthe* (Minack), *Much Ado About Nothing* (RSC Swan), *Rapunzel, Romeo and Juliet, Passion of Christ, Grimms Tales, Measure for Measure* (Creation Theatre), *Taming of the Shrew, Romeo and Juliet* (Guildford Shakespeare), *Ma Kelly, 1936* (Attic Theatre), sets at the National Film School, *Fresh Festival* (Colchester Mercury), *Larkrise and Candleford* (Oxford School of Drama). Assisting credits include *The Wizard of Oz, Carmen Jones* (Royal Festival Hall), *Merchant of Venice* (Galaxy Theatre, Tokyo), *The Tempest* (Tara Arts), *Journey's End, Wedding Day at the Cro-Magnons* (Colchester Mercury).

Lucy designs in two and three dimensions; she designed the logo, website and all production posters for Jericho. She continues to design the biannual cover for the international poetry magazine *Modern Poetry in Translation.* www.lucywilkinson.co.uk

Introduction

The John Donne of this play was a minor figure at best in English cultural life; an attendant lord, peripheral to the principal action. In court society he had achieved some notoriety for a colourful early life and for his distinctive lyrics, but in the age of Bacon, Jonson, Shakespeare and others he was not considered especially noteworthy. It was only in his later life as a cleric that he became famous. By his death he had achieved renown as the greatest preacher of his age, and his sermons – attended by packed crowds in his lifetime – sold in print like hot cakes. It was as a by-product of this fame that his son, looking to cash in, printed also the poems for which we chiefly know him, and which Donne himself ironically would have preferred to keep private.

Yet in 1611, when the action of the play is set, John Donne felt his public life to be essentially over. A decade after a scandalous fall from grace, the new monarch and a new court had done little to restore his fortunes. The disgrace still dogged him: the waspish, ambitious libertine of famed Catholic merchant stock had married, clandestinely, the daughter of a Protestant English aristocrat. Such things were simply not acceptable, and if the younger Donne and his new bride had believed that with time the ignominy would fade they became sadly disillusioned. The court career that had begun so promisingly was finished, never to be regained, and the couple and their rapidly expanding family found themselves in effective exile in the Surrey countryside.

At least his friends did not desert him, and he had a talent for making more. Some had sufficient influence and funds to keep the family afloat. The Bedford family, the Doncasters, the Drurys; these were among the most powerful in the land, and though they could not undo the sins of the past they could temper the hardships of the present. Other friends supplied intellectual and artistic stimulation: regular and convivial meetings with Ben Jonson, Inigo Jones, Francis Bacon and other literary lights of the capital supplied some comfort and allowed him an audience for his songs and poems. His was a radical new informal voice; intimate, colloquial, sexual, metrically rebellious and conceptually dense. The songs were printed and sung in well-off households while the lyrics circulated widely in manuscript, and both were especially popular among women. By the time the new Bible was printed Donne was the lyricist most favoured by composers and musicians – more of them set his words than those of any other poet of the time. It was a reputation he viewed uneasily, enjoying the praise of his peers yet ambivalent about the recognition his writing began to bring him. He knew enough by now to be wary of fame.

At the same time, a burgeoning interest in the new theology brought Donne ever closer to church circles. He engaged in pamphlet debates, usually as ghostwriter for various clergy, and wrote a few well-received tracts of his own. He learned Hebrew, and associated with some of the men who translated the King James Bible. His talent in this area did not go unnoticed, and against all odds it began to be hinted that the reprobate might yet make a cleric. As had become his habit, the formerly impetuous courtier was hesitant in the face of such a choice. His family was not only Catholic but notoriously so: he was a descendant of Thomas More who still kept the martyr's severed head as an heirloom, and his uncle Jasper Heywood had introduced Jesuitism to an England in which Popery was punishable with torture. A handful of years after the Gunpowder Plot, suspicion of those from Catholic heritage ran high. Nor was his own personal history notable thus far for its religiosity. The risk of ridicule and even outrage at a move towards an ecclesiastical career was real, and Donne was well aware that a second dishonour would ostracise and impoverish him permanently. Finally, this decision was for him not only a matter of advancement and security: he was serious enough in matters of the soul to doubt his own motives in such a case. There was much reason for caution.

Yet the world around him was changing, and nowhere more remarkably than in the churches of northern Europe. The Protestant revolution that the English had initially joined because it permitted a petulant king a divorce had come to be embedded more fundamentally in the fabric of their lives than anyone could have imagined. The universe was now a more individual, interior cosmos, in which the earth was no longer central and relationships with the divine were becoming ever more private and personal. In such an environment, regret and repentance were a potent currency, and new kinds of imagery were emerging, based no longer on icons of the general but on symbols of the particular. The emphasis of faith had shifted from the social to the personal life, summed up in the newfangled literary genre of biography, the first contemporary subject of which was none other than John Donne.

In such an atmosphere Donne was a perfect example of the new faith – so long as he could be manoeuvred safely into the side-channel of the St Paul's Deanery, where he could be both highly visible yet remain relatively junior in church hierarchy. He was the reformed sinner, a Catholic on the road to an Anglican Damascus. He became an emblem of the age.

Such a poet as Donne was not unaware of this new identity as a trope in the larger political scheme, and he accepted the role wryly. His great theme of choice in his writing is the microcosm; the notion by which all that exists is an echo and an imitation of all else. Tears are seas, eyes are suns, ideas are universes, and everything and nothing are indistinguishable. In such a plan Donne himself was already an image in someone else's poem, and not least in God's own project. To be thought so in his daily life was simply to say out loud what he believed already, and this he did with astonishing vigour in several hundred sermons – including his last, delivered by him as his own funeral address, days before he died in 1631.

Donne's life bridged the great years of the English Renaissance. It turned on the accession of the Stuart monarchy, whose kings he came to serve, and on the radical cultural and linguistic changes he helped to shape. He was that type we in retrospect would call a 'Renaissance man', a description he would have recognised more than many in the period, if only for the extraordinary acts of reinvention that punctuated his life. He never really ceased to be an outsider, despite his intimacy with the great institutions of the age, and it may be this that contributes to the startling sense of modernity his writing holds. He is never where we expect him to be, and he continually leaps out at us, making us look at the world differently, refusing to let us off the hook; the trickster poet who became a priest.

Jonathan Holmes
May 2011

Inigo Jones costume designs for
Love Freed from Ignorance and Folly

Into Thy Hands

Synopsis

The play is about faith, sex and the translation of the Bible. Set exactly four hundred years ago in 1610–11, it is centred around John Donne and his parallel roles as the first English translator of Galileo, accomplice in the translation of the *Song of Solomon* and as the most popular songwriter of the English court.

Persons of the play

John Donne

Born into a notable Catholic family in 1572, he was a descendant of Thomas More. In childhood he suffered the deaths of his father and all but two of his siblings; as a teenager his remaining brother died in gaol awaiting trial for treason. He attended Oxford, Cambridge and the Inns of Court in London, but was prevented from graduating from any due to his Catholic heritage. He became a soldier, fighting alongside Essex and Ralegh; a civil servant, rising to Secretary to the Lord Keeper; a popular courtier, wit, and twice a Member of Parliament. His scandalous marriage ruined him, and he was exiled to Croydon for a decade, where he became expert in theology and the natural sciences and wrote much of the poetry that would make him posthumously famous. By 1610 he was known chiefly for his colourful past, his political tracts and his lyrics, which were made into popular songs of the time. Through his diligent flattery of patrons he worked himself back into favour, was eventually ordained in 1615 and appointed Dean of St Paul's Cathedral in 1621. Ill for most of the second half of his life, he died in 1631 after preaching his own funeral sermon.

Ann Donne, née More

Daughter of a powerful landowning aristocrat, George More, Donne was originally her tutor. After falling in love and eloping, Donne's burgeoning political career was ruined and he was gaoled for a short time. Subsequently they lived in poverty, excluded from the court for a decade. Despite this, all indications are that it was a successful and happy marriage, producing fourteen children. After her death in 1617 Donne lived alone for the rest of his life.

Lucy Russell, Countess of Bedford
One of the most powerful women of the English Renaissance, counted second only to Queen Anne in influence. A famous patron of poets (Drayton, Donne, Jonson) and musicians (Dowland, Gibbons), she was also an intellectual, a poet, an able developer of her husband's property and a shrewd political operator. She died in 1627, a few weeks after her husband Edward, who was ten years her senior and invalided by a stroke in the 1600s.

Lady Magdalene Danvers, formerly Herbert
Chiefly remembered today as the mother of the poet George Herbert, Magdalene was a beautiful and formidable presence in early Jacobean England. She bore ten children for her first husband, after which he expired. Following a suitable mourning period she married Sir John Danvers, a wealthy aristocrat twenty-five years her junior. She and Donne were close friends for over two decades, and in 1626 he preached her funeral sermon.

Sir Henry Wotton
A clever and adventurous man, Wotton had been friends with Donne since their university days. For most of his professional life he was ambassador to Venice, where he cultivated friendships with most of the major artistic and intellectual figures of his age, including Monteverdi, Galileo, Sarpi and Kepler. He died in retirement at Eton in 1638, in the midst of preparing a biography of Donne.

Lancelot Andrewes

Something of a celebrity at the courts of both Elizabeth and James, he was the pre-eminent preacher and an influential intellectual of the time. He held a succession of lofty ecclesiastical positions and was in charge of the translation of the Bible. As such, he is to be counted among the most important literary and theological figures in English history. He died in 1626.

John Layfield

Another learned cleric, he was Donne's tutor in Hebrew at the time of his work with Andrewes on the authorised translation. He travelled widely, including to the Indies, where his accounts of the New World had a direct influence on his translation of Genesis. He died in 1616.

James VI (of Scotland) and I (of England)

Shrewd, aloof, intelligent, bisexual and politically astute, James maintained power and peace largely through calculated inactivity and astute deployment of propaganda, of which the authorised Bible was probably the most daring stroke. His death in 1625 left England both dynastically secure after the uncertainty of Elizabeth's time while also politically retrograde in the Stuart insistence on personal rule and the irrelevance of Parliament.

Alfonso Ferrabosco (the younger)

A successful composer and son of an Italian musician, Ferrabosco is known to us principally for his many collaborations with Ben Jonson and Inigo Jones. He died in 1628.

Characters

John Donne
Ann Donne
Lucy Russell, *Countess of Bedford*
Lady Magdalene Danvers
Sir Henry Wotton
Lancelot Andrewes
John Layfield
James VI *(of Scotland) and* **I** *(of England)*
Alfonso Ferrabosco
Esther

Prologue

The audience enter to **Ann Donne**, *reading. After a moment,* **John Donne** *steps from the audience.*

John (*addressing the audience directly*)   This is nature's nest of boxes. The heavens contain the earth, the earth cities, the cities people. The common centre to them all is decay and ruin. Only that survives which was never made – that song, which is the very voice of God.

King David said that when people picture an idea in the mind's eye it is like a waking dream, for the imagination is the seat, the scene, the theatre of dreams. This theatre, our imagination, is the place where we sit and see God. It is the whole world, the whole house and frame of nature. Our medium, our mirror, is the book of creatures, and our light is the light of natural reason. David compasses this world and finds God everywhere, and says at last 'whither shall I fly from thy presence? If I ascend into heaven thou art there; if I take the wings of the morning, and dwell in the uttermost parts of the sea, there thy right hand shall hold me, and lead me.'

The whole frame of the world is the theatre and every creature is the stage, the mirror, in which we may see God. All things that are, are equally removed from being nothing, and whatsoever hath any being is by that being a mirror in which we see God, who is the root and the fountain of all. The whole frame of nature is the theatre, the whole volume of creatures is the mirror, and the light of natural reason is our light.

And since, then, at this time I am upon that stage, you may be content to hear me.

Ann   I like it.

John   I'm not sure. Too many jostling conceits. I don't know if it's a good enough beginning.

Ann   Oh, it will serve. When do you give it?

John   Tomorrow night, at Lincoln's Inn.

Ann   They will love you, as always. As I do, always.

John   And I you, my beautiful wife. And I you.

Ann *slips from his grasp and exits,* **John** *sits and buries his head in his hands. He remains so until* **Magdalene** *arrests his attention in the next scene.*

Act One

Scene One

The house of **Magdalene Danvers**, *Chiswick.*

The lady of the house enters, bearing a bowl of water, and sits on a stool. **John** *kisses her, then turns to begin washing her feet and legs.*

Magdalene A good speech, John. It was taken well.

John Thank you, Magdalene. I was glad to see you there. I did not know you had returned.

Magdalene Yes, it was rather a long honeymoon, but then I doubt I shall have another. I missed you.

John I'm sure you had many more pressing considerations than my poor self.

Magdalene Are you jealous?

John The Lord Danvers is respected across the town. In some quarters he is even supposed to have begun shaving.

Magdalene Come, you can do better than that, John. Show me a woman of fifty who would refuse her bed to a handsome nobleman of twenty, and I'll show you a corpse from the waist down.

John Just don't wear the lad out, Magdalene.

Magdalene No danger of that. He bears up very well, in fact.

John How does young George feel about his new father?

Magdalene Envious, of course.

John Poor boy.

Magdalene Yes. Your mother remarried youthfully, did she not? Oh, my poor Jack, are you feeling abandoned? Come to mother Magdalene. (*Pulls him to her, then pushes him back* *again.*) No, wait – have you thought on what we discussed before my marriage?

John   I have.

Magdalene   And?

John   No.

Magdalene   Foolish.

John   Probably.

Magdalene   Certainly.

John   But honest.

Magdalene   Unfortunate. Where will honesty get you in this corrupt world?

John   Heaven, or so I'm told.

Magdalene   Don't hold your breath. And meanwhile you've a family to tend. What of them?

John   They won't benefit from hypocrisy.

Magdalene   Of course they'll benefit, don't be pompous. They will have a living and Ann will have a home, away from that Croydon craphole. (*Provocatively.*) The bosom of the church. Think on it.

John   Oh, I do, Magdalene.

Magdalene   So what is the objection? You'd be good at it. You talk well. And a new Bible from which to preach. You could help people. You'd like that.

John   Yes.

Magdalene   Pride, John. Think of your daughters. The church offers security. Refuge.

John   It is more than that. It is a vocation. A relationship with God.

Magdalene   We all have that! He is inside us all, is he not?

John   You are whimsical, this evening.

Magdalene   For God's sake! The remedy is in your own hands. The king himself has offered you a living.

John   I've booked passage with Drury, we're to –

Magdalene   Oh, stop it John! A gentleman's companion? Whoring yourself body and mind to the peerage? Is this what you want? In God's name, why not the church?

John   Because that *would* be whoring! It needs to live here. (*Taps his heart.*) I cannot feel God inside me.

Magdalene   What do you expect? St Peter himself to pop up and give you the keys to the kingdom?

John   There must be something *heard*! I can't do it in silence. (*Soft.*) That would be too terrible.

Magdalene   Hear me, then. Would every son of mine could enter the church and so be safe. It is a sanctuary; accept its hospitality.

John   No. Not yet. Not while the world spins so.

Magdalene   John, you are not cut out for this world, accept it. You think to keep on selling songs and bending for rich fools?

John   We sing not only to men, but to God. We are his echo. I hope only to hear him myself, one day.

Magdalene   He enters the silences of our mind, where we hear him not. Pay attention and you may yet have your calling. In fact, now that I think of it, are you sure you aren't a little deaf?

John   No. I am not sure. I am unsure, indeed, of everything.

Magdalene   Become sure. Your family's health will not wait on your indulgence.

John   You are a harsh tutor, mother Mary.

Magdalene   I am frustrated by sloth, son John.

He kisses her.

John   Am I forgiven?

Magdalene   You are – so long as my Lord Danvers is absent, that is.

John   I must thank the boy for my good fortune.

Magdalene   No, you must thank me. But it grows late, my friend, and Ann will be waiting. You should go.

John   Churches, wives and daughters! You know how to kill an evening, Lady Danvers.

Magdalene   I love you, John. But don't waste your life in the closets of the gentry.

Magdalene *exits. Stagehands enter and begin organising the stage for a masque.* **John** *steps aside and watches. The boxes are revealed to contain stage furniture; the papers are scripts; the maps become diagrams of Inigo Jones' elaborate sets. And so forth.*

Scene Two

A rehearsal at Whitehall, observed by **John**. *A lutenist plays under the direction of* **Alfonso Ferrabosco**, *who speaks with a suspiciously pronounced Italian accent. Three women, including* **Lucy**, *enter and dance. They wear dresses open at the front, designed to reveal their breasts, though thin scarves now cover their modesty. They falter and the music stops.*

Ferrabosco   God's teeth, can you not keep some kind of time? Counting to four is all that is required!

Lucy   Signor Ferrabosco, need I remind you once again to whom you speak? It is I who decide the time.

Ferrabosco   Forgive me. My Lady Bedford, my fullest apologies. It is the strain of the hour.

Lucy   You are forgiven, Signor, but for the last time. Do you think it is enjoyable for us, to be half-naked in this draughty barn in December?

Ferrabosco   My lady, I apologise once again. It is Mr Jones' idea.

Lucy   Yes, I know. Does he think we are columns to be draped? Or are we the elements of his latest architectural innovation? Cities are not only stone, but also flesh. These are not marble, you know. I shall speak to Mr Jones; this is the last time we are to be so revealed.

Ferrabosco   I am rebuked.

Lucy   You are needed elsewhere. Attend to the tuning.

Ferrabosco *exits*.

Lucy (*to* **John**, *observing*)   John, don't skulk.

John   My Lady.

Lucy (*beginning to change, deliberately facing* **John**)   And you needn't avert your eyes. I'm quite sure this is not the first bosom you have seen, though I grant it may be the finest.

She kisses him, forcefully but not passionately.

John   How is the entertainment proceeding?

Lucy   Coldly. While Master Inigo warms himself in a Cheapside tavern we actors shiver here with his invention. But how are you, John?

John   Well. I am favoured by the Viscount. We leave for France in the new year.

Lucy   But three months? My cousin Drury was ever hasty. And he's your latest sponsor, is he, now that I have less gold to fling at you?

John   My lady, you will for ever be queen of my affections.

Lucy   Affection, John? Do I warrant no further? My dog provides affection. Your ardour has cooled since our time at Twickenham.

John   Your ladyship shall have my love always.

Lucy   You disappoint me. I stand before you like a painted whore, all agog and aglow, and you talk to me like a maiden aunt.

John   Your ladyship –

Lucy   Fie, John, fie! What of truth, man? What of your fervour for revelation? You were not always so circumspect, nor so flat at the sight of my nakedness.

John   The truth –

Lucy   Eludes you. As always, perhaps.

John   Lucy, I do not come –

Lucy   You need not tell me that.

John   – to quarrel, but to beg your forgiveness and good grace. My daughter is unwell.

Lucy   Oh.

Pause.

Which?

John   Your goddaughter. My wife and I – can you visit, Lucy?

Lucy   I shall try, John. When this foolery permits.

John   Thank you. And, one thing further. May I call?

Lucy   The key is yours, John. Always has been. You need only turn the lock.

She turns back to the stage and completes her toilet. **John** *bows as the other women leave.*

Enter **Sir Henry Wotton.**

Henry   Jack! Here you are. How are you, boy? My Lady Bedford, forgive me – I did not recognise you.

John   Henry! Welcome. You received my letter?

Lucy   Ambassador, it is I who should excuse my costume. Had you arrived minutes earlier you would have seen more than just gaudy colours.

Henry   I am ever late, my Lady. Yes, Jack, it arrived safely.

Lucy   And what wonders do you bring from Venice, Lord Wotton?

Henry   My lady, a most remarkable device, which is shaking the foundations of Rome itself.

He produces telescope.

Lucy   It is a tube.

Henry   Yes, my lady, but see: it extends. It removes distance and brings truth closer.

Lucy   I have heard such claims before from excited men; always they ended in disappointment. Gentlemen, I must leave you. John, I will come. My regards to Ann.

She exits.

John   I miss her.

Henry   I, too. John, the world is turned upside down by this tube.

John   I fear you are looking through the wrong end. Henry, it is not the tube causing the disturbance, it is what can be seen through it. The tube is a mere vehicle.

Henry   Indeed! You've read the Italian?

John   I've read the German. How is he, do you know?

Henry   Kepler? Ailing. And railing at the world. He commends your book. Particularly the bits you stole from him.

John   I'm flattered.

Henry   John there is another you should read, by the Italian. I have two copies, one for the King and the other for you. He has caused quite a stir and might yet go the way of Copernicus. With him and Kepler both churches are shivering in the draught of a newly opened door.

John   We still suffer from the squall of the last reformation; there shall not be another in our lifetimes. Bellarmine knows better.

Henry   It may not be up to him. There are other Cardinals in Rome, who take scripture more literally than he.

John   It's a theme of the times. Have you heard the new Bible is near complete?

Henry   Yes. The 'authorised' version. You can imagine how that's been received in Rome; after all, who else can authorise a Bible bar a pope? God? Have you a hand in it?

John   Indirectly. I advise one of the translators on the Song of Songs.

Henry   Do you now? And what does Reverend Andrewes think of that?

John   We have not sought to trouble him with the knowledge.

Henry   I'll bet you haven't. And I met Ferrabosco on the way in; the plucker says you're writing songs for him. How do you square that with your scholarship?

John   The Song of Songs is rendered into English; my lyrics are rendered into song. It is all one music, Henry, all the voice of God.

Henry   That would explain why all the ladies of court have copies, and none of the men.

John   I write songs for women to sing. The Song of Songs is a woman's song.

Henry   What a coincidence. And they said you were for the church. You!

John   Diplomacy has made you cynical.

Henry   No, the world has made me cynical. Diplomacy has made me rich.

John   You've not mentioned the verse I sent you.

Henry   I'm waiting for better surroundings. 'For God's sake hold thy tongue, and let me love.' It's a bit forceful, don't you think?

John   We've flirted long enough.

Henry   An oath? In the first line? A command? You'll be thought vulgar, *amateur*.

John   I am! Common and loving, that's exactly right.

Henry   You should instead pay a little attention to this new science. Maybe a pamphlet? Translate the Italian, Jack; it's a better use of your time. The waves it raises will swamp a wilderness of Bibles.

John   I've missed you, Henry. How are you, really?

Henry   Well. Very well. Venice is a wonder. The most perfect city there's ever been; a marine republic of rivers and reeds. I can't begin to describe it to you, Jack. Come back with me in the spring?

John   I need a living. I can't. I wish I could. I envy you.

Henry   Lying around for the good of the country? Not a bad life, I'll grant you.

John   You have nothing, in your gift?

Henry   I'm sorry, old friend. If I did –

John   Come on, let's have a drink. The world may be turning but it's still awfully dry.

They exit.

Scene Three

*The **Donnes'** cramped Elizabethan house. **Ann** and **Magdalene** enter, talking.*

Ann   For you I'm always free.

Magdalene   Bless you. I know how tired you must be. Now, Ann –

Ann   He won't do it.

Kisses her lightly.

Before you start.

Magdalene   He must.

Ann   You don't understand; it would break his mother's heart. This new church killed one son, now it is to buy the other?

Magdalene (*kisses **Ann**'s forehead*)   And what of *your* sons, Ann?

Ann   We cope.

Magdalene   Come on. There won't be another court appointment. You want him to continue pandering to lordly blockheads into his dotage?

Ann   It must be his choice.

Magdalene   Why? They are your children too. What do you want, Ann?

Ann   I want peace. I want to be less – public.

Magdalene   You can have it.

Ann   I wonder, sometimes, what I should do if he died.

Magdalene   Don't. You're beautiful, Ann, and young. You'd remarry, as I did.

Ann   I would not wish to.

Magdalene   What idiot dreamers you both are! Then you would starve.

Ann   Why should my future depend on a husband? Why should I not be alone, if I choose?

Magdalene   You know why. You were formerly Lady Ann More, with a glittering life ahead. Now you are merely Mrs Ann Donne – Mrs Undonne. That was your wifely choice. Chattels are not permitted independence.

Ann   I do not accept it.

Magdalene   It does not matter.

Ann   It matters to me.

Magdalene   Then you will not matter, either.

Ann   I think, sometimes, it would be a relief not to matter. To be nobody.

Magdalene   So do we all. And it will come, in time. There is no need to hasten to the door; the key is inbuilt.

There is a knock, which startles, then amuses them.

Ann   Well, I'd better answer. (**Lucy** *enters.*) Lady Bedford! You are most welcome, forgive me. John is not yet returned from court.

Lucy   Yes, I left him there. My Lady Danvers, what a nice surprise!

Magdalene   Lady Bedford, I am honoured.

Lucy   Please don't disturb yourselves. I will be only a moment. Ann, how is the child? John told me.

Ann   She sleeps, my Lady. This winter is not kind to us; the children do not have enough dry air.

Lucy   You have six, now?

Ann   We baptised the seventh a month ago.

Lucy   Seven. And Magdalene, you have eight?

Magdalene   Ten, my Lady.

Lucy   I have none. My poets are my children, my husband says. (*Corrects herself.*) Used to say. So in a sense I am your mother-in-law.

Ann   We are grateful.

Lucy   You are fertile, Ann. That is your reward.

Ann   We are blessed, my Lady. And . . .

Lucy   And?

Ann   And yet. A child each year since marriage and John out of favour for the marrying. We receive nothing from my father. And here we are, far from court, in our thin little house. Often John is sick, yet he studies more than ever.

Lucy   Life is hard, is it not?

Magdalene   It is.

Ann   My Lady, I mean not to complain. I have not my husband's tongue.

Lucy   Indeed, he is famous for it. I can testify personally to its efficacy.

Magdalene   Ha!

Ann   My Lady.

Lucy   Yes, that was unworthy. Show me my Lucy, Ann.

Ann   She is sleeping for the first time in two days. It would be better she were not disturbed.

Lucy   I see.

Pause.

Can I look in on her at least?

Ann   She is in here.

Opens door.

Lucy   She is still so small. Thank you, Ann. I hope to return when she is improved.

Ann   You will always be welcome, my Lady.

Lucy   Look after your family, Ann. They are beautiful. And so are you.

Ann   My Lady.

Lucy   Lady Danvers.

Magdalene   My Lady.

Lucy *exits*.

Magdalene (*half to herself*)   Now what does she want? That was not Lucy you showed her, Ann.

Ann   Was it not? I get confused, you know. Oh, I don't know if I can bear being a vicar's wife.

Magdalene   That's the spirit! Shock 'em all; they'll soon leave you alone.

Ann   Do you think?

Magdalene   Of course. You need to turn your backs to be talked about behind them. Trust me, you'll be ostracised in no time.

Ann   I'll drink to that.

They do.

Scene Four

An antechamber at Westminster. **Andrewes** *and* **Layfield**, *working on translation of the Bible.* **John** *enters and once again observes from one side; he is waiting for* **Layfield**.

Andrewes   Kiss me!

Layfield   It has to be.

Andrewes   It cannot.

Layfield   It is imperative –

Andrewes   It is the first line –

Layfield   Followed by the vocative.

Andrewes   It is a female!

Layfield   It is a song!

Andrewes   Canticle.

Layfield   Canticle, then.

Andrewes   Canticle, indeed.

Layfield   But still, a song.

Andrewes   In the abstract.

Layfield   In the material. It is here present.

Andrewes   And will be so henceforth, in the hands of priests across the land. Kiss me!

Layfield   Thus, imperative!

Andrewes   Thus, passive.

Layfield   It is a commandment. It is truth. It is Divine.

Andrewes   It is dangerous. 'The preacher sought to find out acceptable words: and that which was written was upright, *even* the words of truth!'

Layfield   'The words of the wise are as goad.'

Andrewes   Not to sin! Not to fleshly perdition! Layfield, you forget our congregation.

Layfield   Our church.

Andrewes   Church, then. These words, Layfield, will not be spoken only in the universities. They will sound, by decree, from pulpits the breadth of England. They will flood the ears of the sinful and the young. And you say kiss me! A song! Kiss me!

Layfield   And is our purpose not truth?

Andrewes (*rises*)   It is to guide our church along the right path, to lead it not into temptation. Ordinary people do not quibble with tenses, Layfield. They hear 'kiss me' and one thing only appears in their minds. They do not imagine the supplicant imploring her God, they hear uncleanliness. Vice. Abhorrence!

Layfield   The sin of Onan.

Andrewes   Exactly! And is that our purpose? To distract our flock for want of elegant Hebrew?

Layfield   God's voice, Reverend Andrewes, God's voice!

Andrewes   I am not one of your students, Layfield! Do not seek to instruct me on the Song of Songs. I was reading it in four languages when you were mewling at your mother's breast!

Layfield   I am sorry, sir.

Andrewes   God's voice is here revealed in a brightness too blinding for the poor. Our purpose is sureness and certainty; not ambiguity. Now, listen. We need only frame.

Layfield   Frame, sir?

Andrewes   Frame. 'Let him', Layfield. 'Let him kiss me.'

Layfield   'Let him kiss me'?

Andrewes (*standing, puts his arm consolingly around* **Layfield**)   'Let him.' Gentler, dear Layfield. Merciful. 'Let him.' Let our audience think first of men, of a man, of Solomon himself, whose canticle this is. Let Solomon be the kisser, Layfield, for who can sustain unchaste thoughts when his mind is filled with images of Solomon's wise caress?

Layfield   'Let him', then.

Andrewes   Dear Layfield. Let him.

Andrewes *turns to his desk.* **Layfield** *turns to* **John***, who is to one side, trying to eavesdrop. Lighting change.*

Layfield   John, my thanks for coming. I fear I will be in there attending Reverend Andrewes for a while longer.

John   I am in no hurry. Here is the paper you requested.

Gives him a fragment.

Layfield   Thank you. And for letting me see it to start with. It shall go into my tables.

John   How do you proceed?

Layfield   Slowly. We start with 'Let him'. 'Let him kiss me.'

John   But why? It is obviously –

Layfield   It is done.

John   And the second line? As we discussed?

Layfield   He will not listen.

John   He is presumptuous!

Layfield   He is powerful.

John   But, *dodeyka*!

Layfield   You need not tell me.

John   Your *dodim*. Plural. Imperative.

Layfield   What would you have me do?

John   Explain.

Layfield   I have.

John   Justify.

Layfield   I tried.

John   Argue!

Layfield   God's breath, the man reads Hebrew as well as I! What would you employ?

John   Ravish.

Layfield   Ravish? Oh, marvellous.

John   Loving is too . . . sweet. Babes can love. Caressing is close, but insufficient.

Layfield   Ravish?

John   Well, fuck, if you prefer.

Layfield   You push too far!

John   Yes, that too is in the sense: 'Kiss me! Make me drunk with kisses! Fuck me! Thy body is better than wine!'

Layfield   Enough! Remember my cloth!

John   As souls unbodied, bodies unclothed must be.

Layfield   John, our friendship! I cannot hear this!

John   And what of truth, John? What of that? What cares Andrewes of truth?

Layfield   Lower your voice, he'll hear you.

John   What cares he of the calling, the voice of God reaching into the innermost crevice of our being? The song of revelation encircling every tendril of our souls, saturating us with the ever-changing bliss that is to come? Is this not what it is to be ravished?

Layfield   Oh, dear Christ.

John   But what care our betters for this, when they can have 'affection' and – what was it yesterday? – charity. Charity!

Layfield   John, enough now. Reverend Andrewes would stamp upon us both if he heard you. Have you no sense? Go now to your wife and talk to her of ravishing. I must take my leave. We will continue another day. Peace, John.

Turns back to **Andrewes**.

John   Peace.

Pause.

(*to audience*)   Sense? Ravish me! Why do you hold back? I hear your voice in this wilderness. I try so hard to be faithful, and yet . . . Ravish me! Yet you do not.

John *withdraws.*

Layfield *once again approaches* **Andrewes** *and scans the paper.*

Layfield   Embrace?

Andrewes   Embrace! Good.

Layfield   And yet –

Andrewes   Yet what?

Layfield   There is more.

Andrewes   More than?

Layfield   Embrace.

Andrewes   Your meaning?

Layfield   I may embrace you. I may embrace my children.

Andrewes   And you may embrace God.

Layfield   Yes. But the speaker means more. *She* means more.

Andrewes   It is implied.

Layfield   It is. Should it be stated?

Andrewes   How?

Layfield   The meaning is – congress. The verb could be . . . ravish?

Andrewes   Ravish?!

Layfield   It is used in Proverbs: 'Let her breasts satisfy thee at all times and be thou ravished always with her love.'

Andrewes   We are pursuing an allegory of a higher sort, John, with the Canticle. It is neither a proverb nor a marriage vow. We are discussing our relationship with the Almighty.

Layfield   But *habbeq* does denote congress. And the writer –

Andrewes   The writer?

Layfield   The text, that is, specifies the man moves his left arm to her head and the – embrace – is done with his right.

Andrewes   So?

Layfield   Well. Embracing one-armed? It's possible, I suppose. But why be so . . . particular?

Andrewes   Pray tell.

Layfield (*with difficulty*)   Well, unless his arm is doing something . . . else . . . if you see . . . that is . . . *habbeq* implies his arm, or rather his hand, is, well, between and below, if you take my meaning.

Andrewes   For the love of Christ! You want a verse of the Holy Book to read: 'His left arm is under my head and his right is between my legs'?

Layfield   It's what it says!

Andrewes   No, Layfield! It is what you say it says. It is your own mind. Ravishing may be acceptable to the court, but it most certainly is not to me! John, I do not know where these innovations come from. You were not previously so sensuously disposed.

Layfield   They are my own ideas, Lancelot. I consult with none but the Company, and with expert friends of Dr Moreton.

Andrewes   Who are these friends? Poets?

Layfield   All at court are poets these days. It is the fashion.

Andrewes   It is deplorable. And what is that you carry? A fashionable poem?

Layfield (*reluctantly*)   Something from a friend. Not poetry.

Andrewes   May I?

Layfield *passes him the paper*.

Andrewes (*reading aloud*)   'All mankind is of one author, and is one volume; when one man dies, one chapter is not torn out of the book, but translated into a better language.' That's not bad. Is it your own?

Layfield   I wonder if anything is ever one's own.

Andrewes   I approve. Remember, we are not engaged in the fashionable writing of verses, Dr Layfield, nor of song, but of scripture. We heed not Sir Sidney's psalms, nor Mr Drayton's Solomon, but simply the word of God, as witnessed our forefathers in Geneva. As your friend I bid you have care; it would be a shame if you were to become incapable of continuing this privileged work.

Layfield   My apologies, sir. I aim merely for accuracy.

Andrewes   I, too, sir; wherever it does not impede efficacy.

Layfield   I have heard that the king approves the Problems.

Andrewes   He has honoured us with his assent.

Layfield   And the psalms?

Andrewes   I am confident. The king, however, is preoccupied with the Venetian heresy and has not yet supplied his full attention.

Layfield   The tube?

Andrewes   The tube, that seeks to channel God and leave a vacuum in His place. Where once was certainty there is now only void. And they call this knowledge; something replaced with nothing.

Layfield   I have heard it brings the distant close.

Andrewes   Does it? Can it bring the future to us with greater haste? Does it allow me to foresee my death? Or can I now see the past with greater clarity, illuminated by these perambulating moons? Or is it, perhaps, a spectacle grinder's trick, an optical joke?

Layfield   A student of mine, sir, says that it brings us nearer to God. For is it not truer to say that the centre is with God, who is not with us who seek him? That we are forever circling the Divine, tethered by the longest of ropes to the mind of the Lord? Cast out from Eden, we are where He is absent, and He is where we are not.

Andrewes   Is your student another poet, Layfield? Casuistry! The earth is central to the universe, the middle of a capsule of heaven, and we are central to it. We are images of Divinity, small fragments of the mind of God.

Layfield   As the Bible is, too, and yet the meanings needs must escape on the journey from Hebrew to English. Where is the permanence?

Andrewes   Anchored, always, by our faith. Adrift without it. Hold firm to the tiller of your faith, John, lest it be wrenched from you in the peevish flurries of this new alchemy. The world is inconstant; it is God only who is constant, and he will guide us from the earthly to the celestial city, if we give ourselves to him. Those who think eternity can be discerned through a tube are in peril for their souls. Should you encounter anyone preaching such a doctrine, please convey their names to me. Such men are worse than recusants and an example must be made of them.

Layfield   Lancelot, I am sorry if I have angered you. These are troubling times.

Andrewes   My friend, trust in God. That is all we can do. The poets in my father's time did as we do and honoured the work of others; today they gambol in the lines as if the words were inventions merely, and not the messengers of the Lord sent to give illumination in our dark days. Trust to the Word, not to your eyes or the tricks of machines, and seek for constancy. How are we to know ourselves if we fluctuate and shift? Hold firm. Embrace, John, I think, with all its meanings.

They exit.

Scene Five

*Back in **John**'s house. During the masque the boxes had become a rudimentary stage, which now serves for a bed; the large map of the world now becomes a blanket. During **Andrewes**' final speech **John** undresses and gets in bed, where he is joined by **Ann**. **John** has been translating; both he and **Ann** are naked, covered as much by his writing as by the blankets.*

Ann   Mr Donne, you translate simply as *The Messenger*?

John   It bears witness to the truth, Mistress More. At least, that's what Henry and his friend Galileo believe.

Ann   Because Jupiter has moons? Because our moon has mountains four miles high? This is truth?

John   It is what passes for truth in our time. The moons revolve around the planets. The planets revolve around the sun. The universe is all centre, or the centre of the universe is everywhere and the circumference is nowhere.

Ann   I see. Do you mind?

John   Not really. Gorgeous woman, God is in your eyes and your hair, between your beautiful breasts and your delicious thighs. He is in the sparks of your mind and in the voices of our children. He is in the attention we give to the world and in the beauty that is the world's reply. Do I care if it is I or the sun that spins? I care if it disrupts the mind of God – which it cannot.

Ann   So why does the pope care?

John   The pope has a kingdom to run; Galileo would do well to publish elsewhere. But if he is burned there is still Kepler, and if not him, perhaps friend Bacon.

Ann   I think I prefer Kepler. He keeps the harmony of the spheres. I like that; a musical equality, like a choir. And how is poor Layfield?

John   Ah, he is tying himself in knots about sex.

Ann   He is a churchman. That is his job.

John   It is. 'To embrace? To hold? To love? To ravish? To fuck?'

Ann   Oh, to fuck? Above, between, below? And what did he come to?

John   He didn't, of course.

Ann   I prefer ravish.

John   I suspected as much.

Ann   But more research is needed. Let us try friend Henry's modern method, Jack, and experiment. Who know what new worlds we may discover?

John   I see at least seven newly discovered worlds in this little house already.

Ann   And what wonderful little worlds they are, made so cunningly. We are indeed counterfeit creators, for out of nothing came a complete galaxy of worlds, seven crystal spheres singing in harmony; all done, all more, all following their Father.

John   Gorgeous woman, you will either burn, or burn me.

Ann   Gorgeous man, have you your telescope? We should perhaps commence the search for new suns. (*Kisses him.*) Though of course it is not enough only to be scientists, is it?

John   I don't know; there has not been time to find out.

Ann   No indeed. Experimentation can take us only so far. There is more here; a song, no less. This is more like it.

Picks up other papers; reads aloud:

'I am black, and I am beautiful, daughters of Jerusalem.'

John   I couldn't agree, More.

Ann   She is black?

John   So it seems. And beautiful.

Ann   And?

John (*giving in*)   The king's translators would have us believe that the Canticle shows the soiled nature of fallen humanity, yet with a redeeming sheen.

Ann   How dull. Perhaps it is the song of a woman who is black and also beautiful?

John   You'd never survive as an exegete in the universities. You don't overcomplicate enough.

Ann (*sitting up and reading*)   'I am a wall. And my breasts are towers. But for my lover I am a city of peace.' Yes, indeed. Are you don(n)e?

John   Not while I want More.

Ann   And so you are not yourself.

John   How can I be, when my self lives in you? I am in you, and so I am undonne.

Ann   And if I give you More, I am no longer she but am Donne.

John   And so I am More and you are Donne.

Ann   And so you can look after the children tomorrow?

John   And you can sally forth to battle with the court jackals.

Ann   Is it really so bad?

John   No, no. Henry is a good ally.

Ann   Is there no other route? The church?

John   No, my love.

Ann (*kissing him*)   And how is Lucy Bedford?

John   Occupied with fending off Jonson and his tribe.

Ann   Do you miss her?

John   Yes. But it is you I love, always.

Ann   Do you?

John   We had not one another at so cheap a rate as that we should ever be weary of each other. I have been gaoled for you, exiled for you, lost all hope of employment, impoverished and insulted for you. I have forsaken all for you, and would do so again in an instant were it required.

Ann   In this instant?

John   Aye, in a blink, for all eternity is in that instant; past and future being only a dream.

Ann   And so I have loved you always.

John   Even before we met I loved you.

Ann   Before I knew your face or name.

John   Our souls are divine, and unmixed.

Ann   Stretched thin, but never broken.

John   And divinity is a bodily state, for which the angels envy us.

Ann   And to honour the divine we must respect the jealousy of angels.

John   Fulfil our destiny as flesh, in one other's arms.

Ann   Hold each other, for ever, for this is all there is. Touch me, John.

They begin to make love; a baby begins to cry. They stop and look at one another.

Ann   Lucy.

She makes to move.

John   I'll go. Don't go anywhere.

He exits, still naked. There is a pause; **Ann** *alone on the bed, barely covered.* **Lucy** *enters discreetly for a moment, watching* **Ann**.

Lucy   Why, Ann, you look delectable.

Ann (*rushing to wrap herself in a sheet*)   My Lady Bedford, forgive me. I had not expected another visit so soon.

Lucy   It is I who requires forgiveness, Ann. Unannounced and in such haste. But the door was open and, see, I come bearing gifts, like the Greeks: a bottle of fine Spanish brandy.

They both notice it is nearly half empty.

Ah. The journey was cold.

Ann   Thank you. John is – not here.

Lucy   No? How is Lucy?

Ann   She improves. She sleeps most of the time, and is less choleric.

Lucy   I am glad to hear it. It seems such a shame that you live in this manner. All in one room?

Ann   Yes. The children have the other.

Lucy   What can you do with the bed during the day?

Ann   It is rolled away.

Lucy   How charming. And yet a very little could change your circumstance. You must know this?

Ann   John has made his mind up.

Lucy   So Lord Wotton tells me. Quite a price to pay to avoid the church, is it not?

Ann   What can I do for you, Lady Bedford? John may be gone some time.

Lucy   Lucy, please. Ann, I need your help.

Ann   If there is anything I may assist with.

Lucy   I am in need of your particular virtue.

Ann   Please, make me your confidante.

Lucy   It is this masquery of Jonson's. You know of it?

Ann   Something, from John.

Lucy   Is it not shameful, to parade upon a stage like a common player, and naked?

Ann   Naked?

Lucy   From the waist up. The queen herself commands it.

Ann   Before the court?

Lucy   Even so.

Ann   Oh. How can I help?

Lucy   Oh, Ann, you are so young, and I am near thirty. The years are not kind. I need reassurance that my – my shame – is not overwhelming.

Ann   I am quite sure it is not, but how may I convince you?

Lucy   Will you help me with my costume?

Ann   My lady, I am not equipped for such matters.

Lucy (*takes off cloak; she is wearing the Jones costume, without the scarf*)   You are modest. Yet I think you are just the person to help. What do you think?

Ann   Your ladyship is very fair.

Lucy   I see I have not ripened as you have.

Ann   There is still time, is there not?

Lucy   You are beautiful, and young.

Takes the sheet from **Ann**, *exposing her, and covering herself with it.*

Lucy   A whole world in yourself. But there is more.

Ann   Oh?

Lucy   I must sing.

Ann   Oh.

She casually reaches for another bedsheet.

Lucy   I know John writes his verses for you. At least those that aren't written for me, of course. I wish you would rehearse one with me.

Ann   I really think –

Lucy   It is called 'Sweet Stay Awhile'. I have the music.

Ann   I know it.

Lucy   Yes.

She begins singing Dowland's setting of the song; slowly and sensuously.

> Sweet, Stay awhile
> Why do you rise?
> The light that shines
> Comes from your eyes

Beautiful, is it not?

Ann   Yes.

Lucy   You know, you really are beautiful. I can see why John was smitten.

Ann   No, really –

Lucy   You know, I have something else from John. It seems strangely appropriate, given our mutual undress. Would you like to hear?

Ann The children –

Lucy Can wait. Here it is: 'Thy right hand, and cheek, and eye, are like my other hand, and cheek and eye.'

Ann Yes. I know this, too.

Lucy 'Thy body is a paradise, in whose self all pleasure lies.'

Ann Please, I am flattered, but –

Lucy 'My two lips, eyes, thighs, differ from thy two but so, as thine from one another do.'

Ann I am unworthy of your attention.

Lucy 'Oh, no, More, the likeness being such, why should they breast to breast, or thigh to thigh?'

Ann The children will wake.

Lucy 'Likeness begets such strange self-flattery that touching myself, all seems done to thee. Myself I embrace, and mine own hands I kiss, and amorously I thank myself for this.'

Ann I know little of the world, I'm not sure that we should –

Lucy 'Me, in my glass, I call thee, but alas, when I would kiss, tears dim mine eyes and glass.'

Ann Lucy!

Lucy 'Oh, cure this loving madness and restore me, to me; thee, my half, my all, my More.'

She kisses **Ann**. *There is a moment.*

Ann Please, Lady Bedford.

Lucy Well. I think I have learned all I needed. It has been a joy to see you. May I come another time?

Ann Please do.

Lucy   You have been so very kind. I appreciate your assistance. My next performance will be so much richer for it.

Ann   I am glad. Thank you, Lucy.

Lucy   My pleasure. Really. Goodbye, Ann.

She exits. **Ann** *returns to bed and wraps herself in the covers. A beat.* **John** *re-enters.*

John   Lucy is asleep. What's wrong?

Ann   Don't pretend, John. I deserve more.

John   I heard her voice. What did she want?

Ann   You.

John   Why did she not wait?

Ann   Oh, she did not want to *see* you. She wants you. She wants what makes you what you are.

John (*trying to comfort*)   What makes me what I am is you.

Pause.

Ann   She used your poem. The *Sappho*.

John   Oh. She must have had it from Henry. Used?

Ann   You're too careless with your verses. They come back to bite you.

John   Fripperies, all. It is not the songs causing the difficulty. Ann, what happened?

Ann   John, don't ever put me in that position again.

John   I didn't realise –

Ann   Do you hear me? I mean, do you listen? Do you not see how we lie in your hands, how much we trust you not to crush us?

John   I am sorry.

Ann   Are you? Are you really?

John My love. Yes, I am. For everything.

Ann The church, John, not this. I am not a whore.

John Nor I.

Ann That argument is wearing rather thin.

John It is my immortal soul, in the balance.

Ann And what of your mortal family? What of me? Do you know what it means for me? With seven children, no money, in winter? How many of our children has your pride sentenced to death, here in this foetid little outhouse? Every day brings more illness.

John I am trying, Ann. Drury's house will be better.

Ann For how long? Don't you understand? We need a proper living, not another favour. Why won't you do it?

John You know why not.

Ann Conscience? John, there is nothing in the world matters more than our love, more than the love of our children. What says your conscience about that? What else is God's love but this? Hear us – we are His voice. There is no burning bush, and this is surely wilderness enough for anyone.

John I must be – myself

Ann And who is that?

John I wish I knew. But it is not something carved in marble, like an effigy. It is something fluid, something sounded, not cemented. Like a voice, not a text; I exist only as I speak.

Ann And I?

John You are my love; my only constancy. You are all I need in this world. And indeed you may be right. After all, I love you more than I do my own soul.

Ann   I would do anything for you, John, but don't test me.

John   No. Never again. I promise you things will change.

They embrace.

Ann?

Ann   Yes?

John   Do you love me?

Ann   You are my life, and that for which I live. I love you. Just, please, stop being such a fool.

They recline on the bed. Before them the others enter, debating. Throughout the beginning of Scene Six **John** *dresses; once he has finished, so too, discreetly, does* **Ann**.

Scene Six

Whitehall. The daily life of a courtier; loitering in the wake of the king.

Enter **Wotton** *and* **Lady Magdalene**.

Henry   If God is inside us and we are His image, how can the position of the earth affect our centrality to the universe?

Magdalene   Henry, you set too much store by this Italian.

Henry (*kissing her hand*)   My Lady Danvers. It is asserted upon proof.

Magdalene   And what does the musician's son see as proof?

Henry   Observation. Reckoning.

Enter **Andrewes** *and* **Layfield**.

Andrewes   And did he factor his faith into his reckoning?

Layfield   Perhaps he does not presume to know the mind of God.

Andrewes   He presumes sufficiently to redirect the known universe.

Layfield   I mean to say, he restricts himself only to the evidence presented by God to his eyes.

Magdalene   As do we all. Why is he more correct? On what ground does he privilege his interpretive powers above ours?

Henry   Upon the tube. It gives him better sight.

Magdalene   It may give him second sight for all I know, Henry, but I fail to see how orbiting moons demonstrate the sun is the centre of all. I may see the sun circle this world as plainly as he sees his moons spin round Jupiter; why is he right and I wrong?

Layfield   It is by this shown that all does not revolve around the earth, my lady.

Henry   Indeed, one may take this argument as an illumination of God's power, not a refutation.

Andrewes   Sophistry! 'When I consider the heavens, the work of thy fingers, the moon and the stars that you have set in place, what is man?' 'In place', Henry – fixed by God.

Henry   Yet is it not more becoming to God's majesty that his throne and heaven be remoter and grander than we had thought? That we have to stare harder to see it, and we circle Him, rather than He us?

Magdalene   And is this indeed the argument proffered by Signor Galileo?

Henry   He fears the pope too fiercely to write theology.

Andrewes   He fears the truth! The Bible is perfectly clear on this and corresponds with our own observation. It's common sense! Even Bacon agrees.

Magdalene   And Kepler, too. Should we refuse the arguments of two brilliant men in favour of a papist's tubular prevarications?

Henry   I exhort my lady to read *The Messenger* when Donne has finished the translation.

Andrewes   Donne! Is he perhaps your confidant in your translating, John?

Layfield   I have been teaching him Hebrew, Reverend Andrewes.

Andrewes   Have you indeed. And what does he teach you? To think the king wants him for the church!

Enter **John**. *Pause.*

John   Reverend Andrewes.

Magdalene   John, are you persuaded by another Catholic idol? Henry would have you enamoured of a tube.

John   Ah, the sun is lost, and the earth, and no man's wit
   Can well direct him where to look for it.

Magdalene   No man, perhaps.

John   Indeed, there are too few women gazing at the heavens and too many dazzled by the constellations of the court.

Layfield   Come, John, you're translating him, do you believe the man or not?

Andrewes   Careful, Donne.

John   Kepler says we oscillate, Galileo we revolve in perfect circles. Kepler says the universe is a gigantic harmony, imitated by all else; Galileo that it is a discordant void, similarly imitated. I intend to wait until the plates have stopped spinning before looking again at the sky: until then there are troubles enough in our mimicking world.

Andrewes   But, sir, the danger is atheism!

John   God is well equipped to deal with atheists – indeed, only He can change their minds. And besides, I find atheism to be a stringent faith, more suited to solitude than to evangelism.

Andrewes   In our solitude is our danger. It is when we are alone that impure thoughts roam unchecked. We need guidance.

Layfield   Well, I find the man convincing.

Andrewes   Layfield!

Henry   Oh, leave the lad alone, Andrewes. His faith is sound even as his mind is fluid.

Andrewes   And what if his mind overrun the fixity of his faith?

Henry   I never said it was fixed, only that it was sound. It is a river's fixed banks, after all, that cause the waters to flood; 'tis not the water that causes the torrent, but the narrowness of the channel.

Andrewes   Rigour, Wotton. To canalise the river is our purpose.

John   And in doing so what do you control? The waters of the river are never the same, we recognise only the channel itself and call it 'Thames'. We canalise not the river, but our idea of it: we mistake our interference for the truth of the subject itself. It is the same with souls, Andrewes. The more fixity we impose, the more we idolise our intervention rather than loving the waters themselves, and the more likely we make it that these waters shall one day overflow and swamp us all. People must retain their freedom, and we must trust them. In fluidity is our salvation; do not forget it!

Magdalene   Hear, hear! John, you shall be Dr Donne before we know it. You'll see.

Andrewes   You applaud such laxity, madam? Has your boy bride addled your wits wholly? Clarity is what we need, not sophistication. People want decisions, not arguments. And your friend here corrupts where he claims to liberate. Fluidity? Licence! He'll be back harping on ravishing next!

Magdalene   John, what have you been saying?

John   You can't have faith without the body, any more than you can have it without death. And if you have the body then you have all that comes with it –

Henry   John –

John   – appetite –

Henry   John, no –

John   – yes, even communion of the flesh is necessary for faith.

Andrewes   Heresy!

John   Truth!

Layfield   Reverend Andrewes has clarified this in his sermons. Flesh signifies the word, or it represents mortality.

John   Flesh does not 'signify', it does not 'represent' it *is*; it sweats, groans, palpitates, ravishes. The spirit incarnates in love, too, Andrewes, and flesh will fulfil its destiny as flesh. You will not persuade people otherwise. They know their bodies melt and decay and their spirits do not, otherwise the Final Judgement would hold no authority.

Andrewes   There is only the Word, Donne; the Word was with God and the Word is God. Would you alter the Word to suit your doctrine? Then you seek to change the mind of God as much as does Wotton with his wandering moons. You both blaspheme, and you both stand an inch from perdition, not to mention the tower.

John   And what is correct but the truth and the voice of God through the preacher? What is true but ourselves as messengers of truth? Ours is the calling, and the truth will be heard through the spirited voice.

Andrewes It is impure.

John It is loving.

Andrewes Lustful!

John Flesh, Andrewes; you cannot have it without sex. This is what Solomon's song tells us.

Magdalene All this talk of sex! For God's sake calm down, gentlemen.

Andrewes It most certainly does not. It tells us to love God above physical union, above the marriage of individuals.

John Quite the reverse; we love God through our bodies. We might as well try to walk through the city without contending with the houses in our paths. And God cannot be above love because God is love; his spirit witnesses my love for my wife and is in me as I move in her. He is not separate, above, aloof. He is in me; he is me; without me he is not present. Our bodies are marvellous, cruel gifts.

Andrewes I warn you . . .

John (*quoting*) 'My love put his hand into the hole,
   My loins stirred wildly,
   I raised up to open for my love,
   My fingers wet,
   The myrrh flowing sweet
   On the moving bolt.'

Layfield Too much, John!

Henry John, you'll have us all before the Chamber for this. For pity's sake!

Andrewes Listen to your friend, Donne –

John It is His voice! God's voice, coming to us across centuries, allowing us to see the distant past with the clarity of yesterday. Time itself is removed by this Song. Do you see us as isolated and refused? Even the popish stargazer sees the error of that. We are in motion, constant motion,

neither near nor far, always travelling. The universe exists as
a speck in my mind, just as I am a grain within it. Our selves
are larger than the galaxy and smaller than a dot. There is
no distance because there is no time. The present is past,
the past has gone, the future never arrives. Eternity is in
an instant and we exist utterly even as we split. It is a song,
Andrewes, as the text says and as Kepler and the ancients
say; I tune my instrument here at the gate, I put my hand
through the hole and we open to God and to ecstasy; I enter
and we die; all is one moment, one light, one music, one
eternity.

Andrewes   Enough! There is no further argument to have.
This is heresy and I will not listen for one minute more.
You talk of gates? Well, if you are not careful you will very
soon be re-acquainted with the inside of a prison door. Do
you think to be ordained after such a spectacle? Your name
was ever prophetic, Donne; your prospects are finished.
Layfield!

He exits; helplessly, **Layfield** *follows.*

Pause.

Magdalene   You see. A preacher. You can't help it, John.
You're born for it.

John   Written in the stars?

Magdalene   Oh, please. When we look skywards we see
what we look for; that is the only lesson of the tube. The
problem is that when we look up we cease to look at each
other.

Henry   I'd give up all thoughts of a pulpit now, John.

John   Back to prison, as the man says?

Henry   Oh, I don't think so. I'm too useful to the King
on the outside, and he's wary of martyrs these days. Our
Scotsman is shrewd enough not to poke the nest more than
necessary. Remember, it's only five years since the lunatics

tried to blow us all to kingdom come; the last thing that he wants is to start a schism. No, your body is safe; it's your mind you risk.

John   Well, there's no place for me anyway in a church governed by the likes of Andrewes. A synod of clerks, not clerics. They think the soul is an errant schoolchild to be chided into line.

Magdalene   I'm not so sure. I think they know more than you credit them for; they would not else be so scared of you. Search for an independent living, John, and they'll leave you alone. Think on your congregation. And the king still wants you.

Henry   God only knows why. And he may change his mind when he next speaks to Andrewes. Now I really must go. There is much repair work to be done after this afternoon. Goodbye, my Lady Danvers.

Magdalene   Go well, Henry.

Wotton *exits*.

Magdalene   That was a rather passionate show, John. You do realise you're running out of excuses, don't you?

John   I'm not sure if you're my angel or my temptress.

Magdalene   I do hope I'm both. Your guardian temptress. You are beautiful, John.

John   I am foolish. Andrewes is powerful.

Magdalene   But the king likes you. So does young Villiers, and the Drurys. This is a squall, only. It will pass.

John   And you, Magdalene?

Magdalene   Such a glorious sunset we had today. Did you see? I was by an open casement and could not be pulled away. And in winter, too.

John   Ah. Yes, I saw.

Magdalene   It will not be my privilege to bestow patronage for much longer. My own hope for preferment is now in the next world, not this one.

John   It is you who are beautiful, Lady Danvers.

Magdalene   Yes, so armies of poets tell me. But they will not delay my death for one heartbeat, no matter the fervour of the beating. I cannot hold onto what is not mine.

John   No, they won't. Yet think what love can be contained in a single heartbeat! What we lose in extent, we gain in depth. But I did not mean that your face was fair, though I have seen none fairer. I meant your soul. You will not, indeed, lack favour in the heart of God.

Magdalene   Perhaps, son John. Perhaps.

John *exits.* **Lucy** *slowly enters.* **Magdalene** *does not initially acknowledge her.*

Magdalene   Is it worth it, do you think? The intriguing, the masquing? The hurt? Does it have any value, finally, or is it merely distraction?

Lucy   It is not given to us to know.

Magdalene   Too easy.

Lucy   Yes, you may be right.

Magdalene   Why did you not intervene?

Lucy   I will be required to, soon enough.

Magdalene   I am sorry for you, Lucy.

Lucy   I have no need of your sorrow, Lady Danvers.

Magdalene   But that is what the world is – sorrow. Don't you think? We have each other, and beyond that there is nothing.

Lucy   Beyond that, there is God.

Magdalene   Is there a difference?

Lucy   We should not desire the world to be other than it is. Then we would feel no need to lament its deficiencies. I try to look forward only to the life to come.

Magdalene   Admirable. Such sentiment may suffice for some, but not for me. You are so very alone.

Lucy   Do not presume my mind is as your own, Magdalene. I have prayer, and I have God.

Magdalene   Lucy, I've known you since you were a girl –

Lucy   Please forgive me. It has been an exhausting day.

Magdalene   Yes. My Lady.

She exits.

Lucy (*sinks to her knees; to audience*)   Why do you never answer? Why? Do I not suffer enough for you? Must there be more? I grieve 'til my heart breaks for the world as it might have been and could never be, and yet I remain wedded to this ruin, never able to leave. How can it be too much and yet not enough, all at the same time? How? Answer me, please!

Scene Seven

The Bedford seat, Woburn Abbey. **Henry** *is brought in by* **Esther**. (**Lucy** *is still to one side, praying.*)

Esther   My Lord Wotton, if it would please you to wait here. My Lady is at prayer.

Henry   Thank you –

Esther   Esther, sir.

Henry   Esther. Thank you, Esther.

Esther *curtseys and leaves.* **Henry** *is alone for a moment. He pulls out a letter and begins to read. Alerted by* **Esther**, **Lucy** *rises.*

Lucy   Sir Henry. How nice to see you. I trust I am not disturbing you?

Henry   Lucy!

Goes to embrace her; she shies away.

Henry   Just catching up on correspondence. You are well?

Lucy   Very, thank you. What can I do for you?

Henry   I think you know. Jack –

Lucy   I will speak to the queen on his behalf.

Henry   Thank you, Lucy.

Lucy   But you must persuade him to be more circumspect. His previous month in gaol cost him a decade of his life in ruined reputation; he cannot afford another.

Henry   No. I will be surprised if he is not for the church, now.

Lucy   Anywhere, so long as he is less unruly.

Henry   Yes. Lucy –

Lucy   Yes, my lord?

Henry   Do you love him?

Lucy   I love my husband.

Henry   Yes.

Lucy   And he loves me.

Henry   I have no doubt.

Lucy   And yet?

Henry   And yet. The Duke. I knew him well . . . before . . .

Lucy   Before? When he could walk, and ride, and talk as other men do? When he could laugh?

Henry   Forgive me; but he cannot father an heir.

Lucy For which I thank him daily. The miracle of birth, it is called, yet every twitching creature on the earth breeds without thought: surely this is the precise opposite of a miracle? Can anything be more vulgar? I am prouder of my unnatural creations, the poets who resemble God in their uncommonality.

Henry I am sorry. I miss him.

Lucy He has gone nowhere, my Lord. He is still present, at home, and he loves me. He understands me, he sees through me, as no other man does – no, not even your faithless friend.

Henry Lucy I meant no offence. I admire the Duke enormously; have done since we were boys. He is a remarkable man.

Lucy He is. That is why I love him.

Henry And him alone?

Lucy Yes.

Henry Lucy, please. I am sorry.

Lucy I am glad for it. You'll forgive me, I'm sure, if I do not see you to the door?

Henry Of course. Goodbye, Lucy.

He leaves.

Lucy Spare me from men of the world! Esther? Esther!

Esther *enters.*

Esther My Lady?

Lucy Assist me.

Begins to get changed.

Esther, do you think me attractive?

Esther   My Lady, you are very beautiful. All the household speaks of it.

Lucy   And if I were not the source of their wages would they still speak so? You may talk freely.

Esther   I would envy your beauty whether paid or not.

Lucy   You are kind, Esther. But I grow old – I am thirty this year. You are very pretty, and thirty must seem a great age to one of fifteen. At least I thought as much when I was your age.

Esther   All the gentlemen love you, my Lady.

Lucy   Yes, but I am rich. Gentlemen love a fortune, and call it fairness. Fairness itself, meanwhile, they call virtue. To be called fair, therefore, one must buy the most expensive fabrics, whilst to be called virtuous one must wear as little of them as fashion and the season permit. One wishes that words would retain their meanings just occasionally. It would be refreshing.

Esther   Yes, my Lady.

Lucy   Thank you, Esther. You may go. Oh, we leave for London tomorrow – you too, this time.

Esther   Yes, my Lady.

Esther *exits.* **Lucy** *turns and walks across the stage.* **Edward** *is sitting motionless in a primitive bath-chair.*

Lucy   Edward, how have you been? I am so sorry to have been away for so long. I missed you so. Jonson has a new masque in which I am to play: 'Love freed from Ignorance and Folly.' If only it were so. The king's Bible comes on apace, though there is much secret scepticism. Wotton is ablaze with heresy; the new science he calls it, by which God himself has been exiled to the periphery of space. How soon before He is pushed off the edge, one wonders? We cling onto a spinning world.

Oh, Edward. If you were only able to accompany me to
court. It is such a pond of sharks. Forgive me, I know it
is selfish of me. I just miss you so. I love you very much,
Edward. Can you hear me? Can you feel this? I hear the
blood humming inside me – can you? I look into the mirror
and I feel I age visibly; decay all around me. Do you see this
in me too? And meanwhile you are unchanging, permanent
– you are my work of art, Edward. Do you still love me as I
love you? Can you hold me? (*Puts one of his arms around her.*)
Can you feel me? (*Puts his other arm beneath her skirt.*) Can you
feel me here? (*Kisses him.*) Edward, I love you so much. You
were always my world. I could not live without you. You are
my husband, always. You are my day and my night. There
will be no-one else. Edward, my love. Edward. Edward.
Edward!

INTERVAL.

Act Two

Scene One

Andrewes *enters and begins to read his Christmas sermon, spotlit.*
Magdalene, **Lucy** *and* **Layfield** *listen from the darkness.*

Andrewes   'The Word was made flesh, and dwelt among us, and we beheld His glory, the glory as of the only-begotten of the Father, full of grace and truth.'

So says John in his Gospel, and so, at this Christmastime, do I remind you of the coming of the Lord into this world of flesh. Always has the Lord existed as Spirit, but it was as a sign of his love for us, who through the sin of Woman are doomed to fleshly decay, that He consented to become carnal, and to live and die as we do. In the scheme of His eternal life His bodily existence was but an instant, a moment of grief, a tiny discord within the celestial harmony. And in choosing this He reminded us that our fleshly existence is but temporary, a fragment of the greater whole which is the eternal life of the spirit. Our flesh is merely a painful flare, a signal that the greater life is imminent. As a candle reminds us of both the sun and of its own unworthiness; as a cup of water tells us both of its own brevity and of the sea beyond – so too do our lives hint at their own poverty and to the eternity that must surely follow.

It is our task today, as with all the days of the year, to honour the sacrifice of our Lord. Our glory lies beyond the flesh in the life that is to come. Our task is to endure the trials of this life and through them to command our flesh, in the glimpses that are permitted us, to bear witness to that greater glory. Our bodies are a messenger from the Lord, a communication of the life to come. We are the Word enfleshed. Remember, the breasts that are full have as great a pleasure in being drawn upon as the child that draws upon them. The sun on our face; this is a gift of God. The ache of hard work; this is His offering. The pain of childbirth; this is His bequest to us. Above all, the despair of suffering and the fatigue of grief – these are the whisper of Salvation, the greatest of all signals of the life that is to come.

Our flesh is a page on which the Lord does write his Word; we are inscribed by His pen, drawn by the divine ink of the Holy Spirit, which if we will allow shall spill forth upon our virgin skin like the waters of baptism, like the refolding Red Sea – yea, like the great Flood itself, purging uncleanliness from the world of our flesh. The Word was made flesh to show us the grandeur of God himself. Let us remember always that this is its purpose, and that all else is temptation. And let us give thanks for our mortality, that shows us every minute the greatness of the glory that is to come. Amen.

The lights illuminate his audience.

Layfield   Bravo, Lancelot! Bravo!

Lucy   Reverend Andrewes, that was marvellous.

Andrewes   My lady, you are too kind. The honour was mine.

Layfield   The king I'm sure will be pleased.

Andrewes   Thank you, John. Lady Danvers, you are silent?

Magdalene   Apologies, Lancelot. I assure you it is awe.

Lucy   Reverend Andrewes, thank you so much for letting us attend your rehearsal; it would be an honour to converse with you at greater length another time.

Andrewes   The honour would be mine. (*He bows.*)

Lucy   Now I am afraid I must leave for my own preparation: forgive me, I must supervise the coming masque.

Magdalene   'Til the evening, Lucy.

Lucy   Magdalene.

She exits.

Andrewes (*bowing again to the retreating* **Lucy**)   Lady
Danvers, I am agog for your response.

Magdalene   Very well. As I understand it, we are to cast off
all appetite and fly free from passion?

Layfield   Lady Danvers, the corruption of the word
passion –

Andrewes   The degradation, he means, of the Passion of
our Lord –

Magdalene   Yes, degradation is a theme of yours.

Layfield   The word 'passion' is not synonymous with
appetite.

Magdalene   Yes! Exactly. It is just that mixture of a
compulsion so strong it terrifies, the moment when love
seems to melt into extinction; this is the passion I feel and
which overcomes, and which you detest – except when it is
restricted to scripture. In the flesh it is corrupt, in the Word,
sacrosanct.

Layfield   It is a debasement of Our Lord's great sacrifice –

Magdalene   Is it? What was the point of the sacrifice if we
cannot see its application to our own life? I'm not interested
in wilderness temptations, you see. I don't need a vicar to tell
me what to think about my body; I know it better than he
does.

Layfield   It is the comparison, Lady Danvers, with our
Lord upon the cross –

Magdalene   Why did he die, Layfield, if not for us? If not to
bring us closer in sympathy?

Andrewes   But you are a woman.

Magdalene   I had noticed. I'm surprised you have.

Andrewes   Please, do not be affronted. Humanity is fallen
because of the actions of a woman. I cannot help it. It is
therefore our duty as we aim for redemption to resist in

particular the female appetites. I am therefore concerned
above all for you.

Magdalene   You mean you're scared of my sex.

Layfield   Not at all –

Magdalene   You admit it yourself! Eve, Delilah, my
namesake – all shaking the foundations. And how? Through
our bodies. You talk of the pleasure of suckling children
– you who will never do so – but what of the pleasures my
breasts provide for my husband?

Layfield   Lady Danvers!

Andrewes   I cannot hear such blasphemy.

Magdalene   Why is it blasphemous?

Andrewes   Because it is a corruption of the purpose
for which your body thrives. This is just what you refuse
to understand, and indeed you are right to say that it is
dangerous. Your body is sacred, a vessel for procreation.
You disgrace yourself by offering it for pleasure only; is it
not demeaning to claim sexual appetite as equal to rearing
a child? Just as to suggest that what you feel is equivalent to
the experiences of Jesus Christ upon the cross. This is not
some simple prejudice we force upon you to keep you in
false awe, this is the truth! It is hard, but it is true.

Magdalene   It's not that simple! No-one's denying the
sanctity of the crucifixion, Lancelot, or of the magnitude
of birth. Yet surely all the experiences of the body must be
equally valid, equally emanating from Divine Will. Why not
acknowledge them all?

Andrewes   I cannot expect you to understand. Experience
is not all of the same order; you would not compare your
affection for a passing acquaintance with your love for your
son. You must relinquish this stubborn hold on your desires;
you will not be happy else.

Magdalene   But – Oh, I cannot argue with you, Lancelot.
Yet I know you are wrong.

Andrewes   We are all Fallen, remember that. Many are the ways in which experience tricks us. But we should not squabble at this holy season, and I have known you too long to court enmity with you, Magdalene. I would be content to continue our conversation another time.

Magdalene   Dismissed then? Well, probably for the best, as you say. You will still see George come the new year?

Andrewes   I look forward to it.

Magdalene   Good. Good morning, clerics.

Layfield   Goodbye.

Andrewes bows, **Magdalene** exits.

Andrewes   Foolish woman! You know she wants her son to enter our Church?

Layfield   Indeed. But she is old.

Andrewes   We are the same age.

Layfield   In spirit, I meant.

Andrewes   John, you have so much to learn. Come, the day is expiring.

They exit.

Scene Two

'*Love Saved from Ignorance and Folly*'. *All except* **Lucy** *are seated, watching.* **Lucy** *performs Love; she should inherit* **Andrewes**' *spotlight, so that when interrupted by the onstage audience she can be veiled in darkness.*

The Masque:

Love (**Lucy**)   Tell me *Monster*, what should move
   Thy despite, thus, against *Love?*
   Is there nothing fair, and good,
   Nothing bright, but burns thy blood?

Still, thou art thy self, and made
All of practice, to invade
Clearest Bosoms. Hath this place
None will pity *Cupid*'s Case?
Are all the gazing Eyes here
Made of Marble? But a Tear,
Though a false one; It may make
Others true Compassion take.
I would tell you all the Story
If I thought you could be sorry.

Ann   It seems love cannot escape, but is doomed for ever to ignorance.

John   If I know Ben it is we who won't escape. We'll be here all night.

Ann   It's already midnight; it won't take much longer.

Henry   God, I hope not. I'm starving. We've been kept waiting since midday with nothing but sugar to suck on.

Magdalene   Why was there such a delay?

Henry   We were attending the Marshal Lavendin. God, what a boring man.

Magdalene   Very pretty, though.

Henry   As a picture, and with as much depth. A frame, colour, the illusion of meaning –

Magdalene   But in the end nothing but sticky cloth. In my experience.

John   And so the queen, forced to wait, was fortifying the players the afternoon long. They can hardly stand.

Ann   Mr Layfield, you do not watch?

Layfield   Madam, it is indecent.

Ann   How so? It is natural. Half the population has them, you know.

Layfield   But they are not for display. They are for God and your husband only to view.

Magdalene   And our children.

Layfield   Yes, and infants, too.

Ann   And our parents, come to think of it.

Layfield   As a babe, yes.

Magdalene   And our sisters, cousins . . .

Ann   Friends, on occasion . . .

Magdalene   Physicians . . .

Ann   Well, depends how well you like your doctor, Magdalene –

Layfield   Yes, yes, they too may see your – your – but not the court! Not in public! It is shameful.

Ann   How does Solomon have it, John? 'How beautiful are thy breasts, my sister, more delicious than wine.'

Layfield   The Song is symbolic –

Magdalene   Symbolic tits? And I thought I'd seen it all.

Ann   'And thy breasts shall be as the clusters of the vine, which I shall suck.'

Layfield   Oh, God.

Henry   Ladies, don't provoke the poor man. Here, Layfield; let's see if we can't forage for some sustenance.

Layfield   Excellent idea.

They exit, **Layfield** *at speed.*

Magdalene   Don't forget the wine!

Ann   Bless him! I didn't think such innocence still existed.

John   You two are irredeemable.

Magdalene   I know. Better than the entertainment, though. Which in contrast is remarkably dull, despite the

flesh on offer. You know the churchmen really should cease
worrying. I don't know how you do it, working on these
things with Jones.

John   Patience. You would have me practise for the church,
remember.

Ann   And this is why I miss you of the cold evenings?

John   I agree. Hopeless. But we must think of the future;
such folly will soon free *our* love, remember? Independence
is all.

Ann   A republican after all! I knew it. Once the Roman
prince is rejected all others must closely follow.

John   Bless you but hush, we can't afford a bloody sedition
trial.

Magdalene   Practising for the church, eh?

John   Enough! Enough. I am in your hands both; be
gentle!

Magdalene   What shall we do with him, Ann?

Ann   Why, keep him for our pleasure, my Lady.

Magdalene   Stay as we are, then.

Love   Ladies, have your looks no power
   To help Love at such an hour?
   Will you lose me thus? adieu,
   Think, what will become of you,
   Who shall praise you, who admire,
   Who shall whisper, by the Fire
   As you stand, soft tales; who bring you
   Pretty News, in Rimes who sing you,
   Who shall bathe him in the streams
   Of your blood, and send you dreams
   Of delight; a world entire
   Within a mind that never tires.

Ann   Mmmmn, dreams of delight. I've had a few of those recently, while you've been away.

John   I must come unexpectedly one day, and wake you so we can enact the rest.

Magdalene   Don't let me disturb you. The Lady Bedford is quite flushed. Do her good.

Ann   It will.

Henry (*re-enters with* **Layfield**)   Success! Viands. Let make a start on all this flesh.

Ann   With pleasure, my lord.

Love   'Tis done, 'tis done. I have found it out,
   Britain's the World, the World without.
   The King's the Eye, as we do call
   The Sun the Eye of this great All.
   And is the Light and Treasure too;
   For 'tis his Wisdom all doth do.

Applause.

Magdalene   Oh, thank the good God that's over.

Henry   Well, the ladies remained vertical after all, the count seemed amused, and we can all go home. Honestly, this charade has nothing on the public playhouse. You know Ferrabosco's man has a play at the Blackfriars?

John   I heard. Shipwreck in the Indies, right?

Henry   *The Sea Venture*, yes. Weren't you supposed to be on that ship?

John   Had we the means, we'd have drowned.

Ann   I knew we were poor for a reason. Light enough to float.

Layfield   I was there.

Magdalene   What was that?

Layfield   On the previous voyage. I was a year in the Indies. A paradise, untrammelled, unblotted. A miniature Eden, set aside by God in a sea of plenty, where innocence still thrives and each day a state of grace exhales from crystal caves. Nothing but simplicity and liberty, as if the first breath of creation still lingered over the isle like mist. A perfect world.

Magdalene   And does this word exist in the west, or in your mind?

John   Magdalene!

Layfield   The answer, Lady Danvers, is both. We can observe nothing without corrupting it with our observation; that is our curse, since Adam. Knowledge is nothing if not knowledge of despair; innocence cannot survive in the face of it. And now the paradise I saw does exist only in my mind, for our discovery of it was its destruction.

Ann   And so paradise is always beyond our knowledge?

Layfield   Our daily tragedy.

John (*looking at* **Ann**)   We create as well as corrupt; that is the consolation of experience. My own paradise is daily made clearer to me; I can imagine nothing better. We lose innocence, and we gain love.

Layfield   I do not know.

Henry (*restoring the mood*)   So, Jack. How'd you like to hear your songs in the playhouse?

John   God forbid. It would be the ruin of me. Enough that Ferrabosco and the rest persist.

Ann   And we'd never see ladies so arrayed; Henry, are you saying that you prefer boys in dresses to the finest ladies of the realm half-out of them?

Layfield   Well it must be preferable to this fashion for revelation. The boys are more circumspect, and somehow more – feminine.

Henry   I disagree. Would Jones could costume all the ladies of Cheapside so. I should have brought the Italian tube; here was a pretty sight for gazing.

Ann   My Lord, I blush. John, take your retrograde friend away!

Layfield   Lord Wotton, I must protest at your –

Magdalene   And here come the liberators of love. My Lady.

Lucy (*drunk, still topless*)   My Lady Danvers. Ann, so delightful to see you here at court.

Layfield (*trying not to look*)   My Lady Bedford, please take my cloak, it is a cold evening.

Lucy   Is it? I feel quite warm. But thank you, Mr Layfield. You are very kind. (*Kisses him.*)

Layfield   Aargh! My lady, I must –

Lucy   John, your wife was a great assistance in my performance.

John   Yes, so I hear.

Lucy   Do you now? Yes, it was her nimble fingers reached the heart of my matter. I had such problems with this attire of Jones's, you see.

John   I am happy that Ann was able to support you.

Lucy   So was I. Very happy. Very.

Ann   I did all I could, my Lady. I am only glad you came.

John   I am sure, that if you needed a glass in which to see yourself again, Ann would be only too pleased to act as your reflection.

Lucy   Indeed. I, too, am glad for it. And for your company, both.

Henry   My Lady, a capital performance, and a most glorious costume. Will you take some wine? Here, Lucy, you need congratulating!

Lucy   My Lords, I fear I am already over-tired, and must retire.

Takes the offered glass anyway, and drains it somewhat unsteadily.

Tired and retire. Oh, I hope you have a pleasant morning, as I see it is now past midnight. John, my regards for your travels. And look to your wife; few know her equal.

John   Thank you, my Lady Bedford. I will do all that you ask, always.

Henry   Allow me to escort you, Lucy, to your carriage.

Lucy   Thank you, thank you, Lord Harry.

They go.

Layfield   Well! Such decadence. I begin to think Lancelot may be right.

Magdalene   Now, Layfield. There is no-one of purer intent than Lady Bedford. There is no cause for scandal. Is there, John?

John   Not at all. My Lady Bedford was assisted in her preparation by Ann.

Magdalene   Was she now?

Ann   I believe I helped her see the part of Love differently.

Magdalene   Which part? No, don't answer that.

Layfield   And to think you consider setting the Song of Songs!

Magdalene   Really?

John   Why not? There's a tradition. Orlando would do it, I think, or perhaps Dowland.

Layfield   The church custom is for boys!

John   So I've heard. Makes no sense, does it?

Ann   It should be a girl, surely?

Layfield   It cannot. It is not possible to have a female sing the sacred canticle and preserve its theological dimension.

Ann   Why not? Because of all those breasts?

Layfield   Because of, er, well the, the, oh, Lord.

John   It would make the point very clearly. Bodies, sex, the soul, all in harmony, all in one voice. A kind of trinity; the corporeal, the spiritual, the communal. God's presence in the body and voice of the woman singing, just as in the man preaching in his pulpit.

Layfield   Oh, please don't start this again!

Magdalene   He has a point, John. It's very late.

Ann   It's all one, Layfield; an expression of the divine, whether worlds spinning or bodies loving or voices calling.

John   It's how God relates to us.

Layfield   Not to me he doesn't. No, don't continue. It's quite enough for one night. I'm not sure I feel at all well.

Andrewes *enters*.

Andrewes   Layfield!

Layfield   Oh no.

Andrewes   What in God's name are you doing here?

John   Be calm, Lancelot. He was invited.

Andrewes   This is no time for frivolity; it is Christmas. John, it's time you are abed.

Magdalene   It is, too.

Ann   Reverend Andrewes, Mr Layfield has conducted himself with decency –

Andrewes   I should hope so. I should have hoped too that he would be somewhere else!

Magdalene   Why are you here, Lancelot?

Andrewes   I attend the king.

Ann   What is wrong with hearing a masque?

Andrewes   It is lascivious.

Ann   Because of the nakedness?

Magdalene   Lancelot believes the female body to be degrading and sinful and not for public show.

Andrewes   Layfield!

Ann   Oh.

Layfield   I am ready, Lancelot.

Ann   But surely it is my body? Mine to do with as I wish?

Andrewes   It is God's, madam. You are only its custodian. And your actions do not occur in isolation; they affect others.

Layfield   He's right, Mistress Donne.

Ann (*thinking it through*)   Nowhere in scripture does it say that I exist to bear children only. Many are the references, in fact, to the pleasure given by the female body, and to the beauty of physical love between men and women. All of this must therefore be sanctioned by God. So where does your authority over my body originate? Certainly you have your opinion, and you may be correct, but it cannot be a commandment.

Andrewes   Woman, have a care –

John   No, you have a care, Lancelot. You would seek to shackle the world to a regime of worship and decree, but happily there is more, always more. No matter the statutes and the edicts you impose, people will always in their vulgarity find joy in the everyday and the inappropriate. Always they will exceed, overflow your intentions, and they will love uncensored and unsanctioned. And I thank God for it.

Ann   'A veiled garden is my sister, my lover,
   A hidden well, a secret spring.
   You are an orchard, a grove
   Of pomegranates,
   You are a fountain in the garden,
   A well of living waters.
   Every inch of you is beautiful,
   My lover,
   My perfect one.'

Does this sound like a degraded body? Does this suggest that physical love is an evil?

Andrewes   There is a moral law, a law of God greater than appetite –

Ann   There is indeed, and I love it too, but I do not speak of appetite, I speak of love. For your moral law to exist there must be real choice in our lives, for where are the ethics in compulsion? If I am constrained by law then my decisions are not my own and I cannot be acting morally. We choose, Reverend Andrewes, and I pray to do so wisely, but I pray most of all for the freedom to do so in the first place.

Andrewes   This place has corrupted you; there will come a day when it shall be prohibited. And I choose, Mistress Donne, not to pollute myself further with your company. Good night, Lady Danvers.

He exits.

Layfield   I should leave too. Good night, ladies. Good night.

John   Good night, my friend.

Layfield *exits.*

Magdalene   I thought you were the sensible one, Ann.

Ann   What have I done?

John   Exactly what you told me not to do.

Ann   But he's just so infuriating.

Magdalene   He is. He was the same as a boy. Peevish little pedant.

John   Don't fret, Ann. No harm done. At least none more than I am responsible for already. He can't be more against us than he was before.

Ann   I think it may be time to go home.

Magdalene   It is time for us all to retire. And besides, all this talk has made me think on my own John. I shall be my husband's dawn chorus, and be home in time to see the sun rise.

Ann   Go well, Magdalene.

John   And take our love with you always.

Magdalene   I always do, John. Good morrow, Ann.

She exits.

Ann   To our waking souls?

John   And our new worlds.

He touches her belly, suggesting pregnancy, and they kiss.

Scene Three

One pageant replaces another. The scenery for the masque becomes, with minimal alteration, that of the court.

Attendant   Wait here.

John *waits as everyone else leaves.*

Attendant (*returns*)   This way.

King James *takes his place on the masque stage, as if performing.* **John** *watches from the 'audience'. Throughout,* **James** *is cordial but obviously dangerous.*

James   Mr Donne. My thanks for your time.

John   Your majesty honours me.

James   Yes I do, don't I? The question is, how do you honour me?

John   In every waking thought I am your subject and servant.

James   Good, good. Do you like the new Bible?

John   It is the most learned of accomplishments.

James   It is. Thanks to Andrewes and to your friend Layfield. Good men.

John   Yes, your majesty.

James   The people now have the comfort of authorised scripture; never changing, always secure. Always faithful. Fidelity is so important, don't you agree?

John   Yes, your majesty. I strive for it in all I do.

James   Quite. Will you take orders?

John   Your majesty flatters me.

James   No. I know your talents, John. I measure accurately. We have this past two years a new Bible, one that will outlast the popish prattle and quite possibly the language. It is my cathedral, my church of words, and it shall endure longer than St Peter's in Rome. We have the beginnings of a clergy of greatness: Andrewes, Moreton, Laud. Has any other nation had churchmen of this degree since the days of your grandfather Thomas More?

John   Indeed, it is a fine group of men.

James   The reformed church, less than a lifetime old, is the envy of the world. The learning of London outdoes Rome: this is the City of God, now. It is the future. Why not join?

John   Your majesty I am unworthy, and the Reverend Andrewes –

James   It is not for you to gauge your worthiness, John. That's vanity. Nor is it wholly the responsibility of Reverend Andrewes, wise though he is. No, I am the judge and I say you are both worthy and ready.

John   I am overwhelmed. If there could be another part I could play –

James   God's body, John, what other priest has your abilities? A lawyer, an expert on popish myth and mystery, a man of science. A lover. Who else is there? The wise fool Bacon? He cares not for souls. You will bring to the church what no-one else is able to.

John   Your majesty, I have a reputation –

James   Damn it, man, so do we all. So did Paul, so did Augustine. You are my Augustine, John, a sinner converted, God's favourite dish. A man adrift, now anchored in the harbour of the church. You will be listened to. You are authentic.

John   I have struggled always, your majesty, with my place in this world.

James   That's honest, John. I admire it. Your family has a fashion for the fire; 'tis good to see you resist.

John   There is not one person in my house well. I have already lost half a child, and my wife has fallen into a sickness that would afflict her much but that the sickness of her children distracts her, of one of which, in good faith, I have not much hope. I flatter myself in this, that I am dying too. Nor can I truly die faster by any waste than by loss of children.

James   Truly, Donne, I am sorry for it.

John   Thank you, your majesty. It had been my hope to think on the priesthood with a calm mind and peaceful heart.

James   You want that which the office confers, before taking it. Don't anticipate, John.

John   No, your majesty.

James   Donne, your uncle opened the Jesuit floodgate to this country. Your brother died a heretic while awaiting the block. Your stepfather was a known papist, your mother remains so. Your Catholic line is sainted in Rome, not least for More's opposition to an English Bible, and your own disputational fame does not quell the clamour. You are very nearly a symbol, Donne; a dangerous occupation in this explosive world. Well, I wish to confirm you in another symbolism, as a reformed soul. Which, happily, you actually are. Aren't you?

John   It brings me such joy that you prefer me so, your majesty. You have my word –

James   I have your flesh also. Don't forget that. I am God's deputy and you will be coined in my image. You will cease these flights of scientific fancy and you will join with Andrewes as one of the pillars of the new church. Am I sufficiently clear? Oh, and you'll have a living for your family for the rest of your life. You can help them, John. I am offering you the keys to a sanctuary for them. A nest. A little world, undisturbed, free from worry, safely cushioned within this larger one of my realm, itself a mirror of Heaven.

John   Your majesty, it grieves me to earn your displeasure so.

James   Calm yourself, John. I am not yet displeased. Be assured. And think on what we have discussed.

John   Your majesty is kind.

James   Yes. But do not mistake; there shall be no other living for you but this. No more favours from the court. It's this, or nothing.

John   Your majesty.

He exits. **Layfield** *emerges.*

James   Well?

Layfield   Yes, your majesty.

James   Yes. Will he be instructed?

Layfield   I think so.

James   I do not trust him.

Layfield   He will be a monument, sire, to your reign. And the appointment will placate the recusants. It is worth it.

James (*leaving*)   I hope so, Layfield. (*Kisses him lightly.*) For your sake.

They exit.

The substantial pageant partly fades.

Scene Four

Andrewes' *study.* **Lucy** *is kneeling before him.*

Andrewes   It is good to see you here, daughter.

Lucy   Reverend Andrewes.

Andrewes   How has it been, since our last meeting?

Lucy   Difficult.

Andrewes   My child.

He waits.

Lucy   Reverend Andrewes. Reverend Andrewes, forgive me, I wondered –

Andrewes   Come, Lady Bedford, please be not afraid to question.

Lucy   Reverend Andrewes, the body is plagued with so many appetites –

Andrewes   It is.

Lucy   They come in ambush, unforewarned, like robbers, the better it seems to compel entry while the mind is distracted.

Andrewes   My Lady, be assured. Our Lord in the wilderness was prey to just such temptations; his example is given to hearten us all.

Lucy   It is a torment.

Andrewes   Suffering is our duty.

Lucy   Why? To what end?

Andrewes   As to the end, that is not given to us to know. Indeed this is the meaning of true faith – complete trust in the guidance of the Christ. As to the 'why', that we know: to renounce all that is worldly and to join with God.

Lucy   You make it sound so simple. And yet it is an agony.

Andrewes   Then release your grip on that which brings anguish.

Lucy   I love him.

Andrewes   God loves you more than this; God is love. Give yourself to him entirely, let him envelop you with his compassion. No earthly experience could be surrogate for this.

Lucy   I must let him go.

Andrewes   Pain exists to lead us to glory.

Lucy   And grief?

Andrewes   Death comes for us all. This knowledge is pain when we do not fully believe; when we give ourselves over it becomes joy, a pure delight to be relieved of a life of care. In the meantime we are alive, but not yet awakened.

Lucy   A dream. Yes, that is sometimes how it feels.

Andrewes   Daughter, you are good. Do not be afraid. Your salvation is assured.

Lucy (*stifling tears*)   You will help me?

Andrewes   Of course. Let go of the babble of this life and listen only to the divine Word. All mankind is of one author, and is one volume; when one man dies, one chapter is not torn out of the book, but translated into a better language. This life is but a means to an end; we are but a means. And it is as a means that we discover meaning. Do you understand?

Lucy   I think so. I want only to be loved.

Andrewes   You are. God loves you. He always has.

Lucy   I do not sense it!

Andrewes   You shall.

Lucy   You will not leave me?

Andrewes   I shall be with you, always.

Lucy   Thank you.

Andrewes (*embracing her, stroking her hair*)   There, there. Let it go. You are loved – never forget it. Let go of him, of all your cares. You are loved.

Lucy   I want it so much.

Andrewes   It will be yours. You are loved. I love you.

Lucy   Oh, God.

Andrewes   I love you.

Lucy   You will stay with me?

Andrewes   I shall be always at your side.

Lucy   You will love me?

Andrewes   I do so already.

Lucy   And I you, Reverend Andrewes.

Andrewes   My dear.

Scene Five

John's *house. Throughout this scene* **Ann** *is in considerable pain; for the first part she is trying very hard to conceal it.*

Enter **Magdalene**.

Magdalene (*removing her cloak*)   Why will he not accept the king's confirmation?

Ann   Unworthiness.

Magdalene   Come on!

Ann   Oh, alright. He mistrusts it.

Magdalene   Why?

Ann   Thinks it's a trap.

Magdalene   How?

Ann   Precisely because it confirms. Fixes him.

Magdalene   And saves you and yours.

Ann   At a cost.

Magdalene   Yes. One worth paying.

Ann   Perhaps.

Magdalene   Wake up, Ann! I know Andrewes is against him, but you're not here to be sacrificed on the altar of his conscience. That's vanity, of a sort. You want to suffer?

Ann   Do I?

Magdalene   it seems so.

Ann   You may be right.

Pause.

Magdalene, I do not think the babe is well.

Magdalene   What?

Ann   I think it is – no longer living.

Magdalene   Why? How long?

Ann   A day. Since John went to court.

Magdalene   It's just the strain. This house. The cold –

Ann   I've been bleeding.

Magdalene   That could be –

Ann   It is not.

Magdalene   It may still be well. Let me see.

Ann   I do not think so.

She lifts her skirt. Underneath, all is bloody.

Magdalene   Oh my God! Why didn't you say?

Ann   To whom could I say it, being alone? Apart from God, whose will it must be.

Magdalene (*taking a bowl of water from the side*)   Ann, we must clean you. You can't sit there in –

Ann   But why it must be His will is best known to Him. He certainly thinks me unworthy of his confidence.

Magdalene   Ann, please –

Ann   No. You say we are in John's hands. I used to think so too. Could he have prevented this? No. Only God. And yet you think John is wrong to be so cautious of embracing Him.

Magdalene   You could have a warmer house, at least. If –

Ann   Could! If! Fairy tales. What there is, I have; what we are, I am. Love, and death. I get one from John, the other from your God. The rest is, as you say, vanity.

Magdalene   *My* God? Please Ann. I am your friend.

Ann   Then do me one courtesy. Do not seek to excuse my suffering with arguments about God. I prefer the pain, if it be true.

Magdalene   Ann, I'm sorry. This is the way the world is.

Ann   Yes, it is. The point is, I realise I do not need to think it more.

Magdalene   Ann. When did this start?

Ann   This morning. I think it is finished. The flow at least has abated.

Magdalene   And?

Ann   It was so tiny. Hard to be sure.

Magdalene   Oh, my dear. My dear friend. Come, you must rest. And we must clean you up.

They begin to clean; **Magdalene** *wraps* **Ann** *in her cloak.* **John** *enters.*

John   Magdalene, what an unexpected pleasure!

Magdalene   I'm just leaving, John. Come here.

John   Oh.

Beat.

Have I offended in some way?

Magdalene   No. Attend to your wife, son John. I must go. Ann, you know I love you.

Ann   I do. Come back soon.

Magdalene   I will. Goodbye, both.

She exits.

John   Goodbye, Lady Danvers. Ann?

Ann   You are late.

John   I am sorry.

Ann   How was the king?

John   He wants me to take orders. He – what is it, Ann?

Ann   John, the baby's gone.

John What?

Ann I miscarried.

John Oh, Jesus.

Ann What are we doing wrong?

John I do not know.

Ann Not a death in ten years of sickness before this. Where has our peace gone?

John My love. Don't talk.

Ann I cannot do this any more.

John My love, my beautiful love.

Ann It is too much pain.

John I know.

Ann The child has not been baptised. Had not. The church would have it he was in sin.

John God would not deny one so eager to meet him.

Ann God? The scripture says –

John Oh, Christ! The scripture is – mistranslated. We cannot know what is in God's mind.

Ann How do we keep going?

John We let go. We . . . dissolve.

Scoops up water from the bowl.

We are as water in the hands of God.

The water seeps through his fingers; he begins to clean her.

Ann And so let us melt?

John And make no noise.

Ann I'm so tired.

John I know.

Ann   I want it to end, the pain.

John   I know. It will.

Ann   I am twenty-nine years old, John. I'm exhausted.

John   I am here. I am here.

Ann   Talk to me.

John (*still cleaning her thighs and legs*)   Let me pour forth
tears before thy face. Thy face coins them, thy stamp they
bear. Fruits of much grief they are. Emblems of More.

Ann   John, I'm frightened.

John   O more than moon, draw not up seas to drown me.
Weep me not dead in thine arms; forbear to teach the sea
what it may do too soon. Let not the wind example find to
do more harm, since thou and I sigh one another's breath.

Ann   Let us melt, and make no noise.

John   You are my self, my haven.

Ann   I? I am a wall. But for my lover I am a city of peace.

John   Still the most. For ever More.

They hold each other. Then **John** *moves aside and exits.*

Scene Six

Ann *is, for once, entirely alone. The stage is bare apart from their
bed, on the end of which* **Ann** *sits throughout. She has recovered,
somewhat, from the previous scene.*

Ann   Well. (*To audience.*) I am not used to speak to you and,
no doubt, you were expecting my husband. He does tend to
monopolise you, but I too have a voice. (*Indicates the remnants
of the masque stage.*) Such folly. The opposite of truth, of love.
(*Begins to undress, but then stops.*) Nakedness is the greatest
costume of all, don't you think?

What I dream happens as surely as that which I see, for
it happens to me. The makings of the mind are as real as
those of the hand; if they were not, it would not please our
Majesties to place us in the gaol and upon the rack until
they be public. Our actions are but the fleshly echoes of
our thoughts, which themselves are the constellations of an
inner universe more vast than anything Galileo can perceive
through his tube. Man is not a little world, he is the greater –
yes, and woman too. If truth is what we seek, we should look
not abroad but inward; all else is but a mirror on a stage.

He did eventually take orders, as you know. It took some
persuasion, but everyone has their price. For John it was
death. For every year he delayed, our poverty killed two
of our children. And the king did not relent. We lost four,
before he accepted. Conscience, or pride? Only you truly
know. When he finally did give in, he was able to wipe the
slate clean. All sins forgiven. Heaven rejoiceth, and we were
invited to all the best banquets.

I never know if you hear. No response. No matter. I suppose
that if you know everything anyway, then all this prattle is
rather embarrassing. And if you do, then this vast inner
world of my mind, this galaxy, is nothing more than a
reflection of what is already in yours. And as this reflection,
too, must be there imagined, our time upon this stage is
but a reflection of a mirror of your mind. A kind of triple
echo, searching for the voice that shapes us. How paltry we
become when you are countenanced; yet how majestic when
you are disavowed.

I often wonder about you as John and I make love. Do you
watch? I suppose you must. Do you condemn the pleasure,
as Andrewes and the others argue? I cannot believe that.
Without the pleasure there would be no propagation. If
you approve, and if you are within us and without us as is
commonly thought, then I am fucking you, am I not? And as
you are in John, too, then you are fucking yourself. No, you
can't dislike the pleasure.

And if all this is true, then every time a child of mine dies, you die too. Every time John is wracked with illness, you suffer too. Either you feel everything, or you feel nothing. And if you feel everything, why do you not stop the pain, as a good God would? No response. But if you feel nothing, you are either indifferent or it is as if you do not exist. Which comes to the same thing. So those are the alternatives: a cruel god or a non-existent god. Which is it? Whose hands am I placed in? What choice must I make?

Your answer came soon enough. As I went into labour there was, this time, too much pain, too much blood, and I saw in John's eyes as he looked at me that the child had died. And as I continued to look his eyes went dead and there was such agony, such torment, and I saw the truth mirrored in his despair; I knew that I was dying too.

Forgive me, John, for leaving you. You are my world.

She sinks back onto the bed, which slowly becomes an open grave; the world map that is the blanket sinking down to form the sides and floor. Other characters, muffled in black, attend the funeral. **John**, *barely able to stand, throws soil onto Ann. A moment of sheer grief.*

Scene Seven

Woburn Abbey. **Lucy** *and* **Henry** *enter a ruined church. Near the front a large crucified Christ hangs from the ceiling as if displaced in a ransack; it is upside down.*

Henry   Still not rebuilt?

Lucy   Too many rivals for the architects' attention.

Pause.

Henry   Andrewes is still here?

Lucy   Should he not be?

Henry   There are other . . . advisors.

Lucy   I cannot think of one.

Pause.

Henry   He is much changed.

Lucy   God changes us all.

Henry   'Twas not ordination altered him, Lucy.

Lucy   I mourned her, too.

Henry   Does he know?

Lucy   I doubt he'd care.

Henry (*looking around*)   Will you have a choir, when it's ready?

Lucy   I think so. Tallis sang here, you know.

Henry   Dowland wants preferment.

Lucy   Dowland is a bore. Dr Andrewes will select the right man, when the time comes.

Henry   You are close.

Lucy   He has shown me things, Henry, I had not previously imagined.

Henry   And there is no room for a rival?

Lucy   I was rejected. Pushed aside. No longer needed.

Henry   Needed more than ever. (*Glances round the church.*)

Lucy   You are a good friend to him, but you are untruthful. These are new times. We have a new Bible, new offices, new accounts. The old world is decaying.

Henry   He still uses the old Bible, did you know? Artfully, of course, making sure the king does not discover it.

Lucy   Dr Andrewes says the old Bible is heretical.

Henry   It's brilliant. So's the new one. They're all wonderful. And at least it's a distraction for the Catholics;

these new 'Protestants' are too busy schisming among themselves.

Lucy   *Them*selves, Henry? And the pyres are not neglected; now we burn women instead.

Henry   The king dislikes witches.

Lucy   The king dislikes my sex, and who is there to defend us, when all the powerful men concur?

Henry   You are powerful, my Lady

Lucy   And I can't get a roof for my church! Don't patronise me, Henry. Influential women are like candles; easily snuffed out, and not very visible in the bonfire of court.

Henry   He misses you.

Lucy   Convenient.

Henry   He is adrift.

Lucy   Trite.

Henry   He is alone.

Lucy   So are we all, in the end.

Henry   He hates his God.

Lucy   Now you're being honest.

Henry   You're pleased?

Lucy   His intelligence has spared him much over the years. It is time he understood.

Henry   He collapsed. He is not himself. She was his world, Lucy. Do not be cruel.

Lucy   The world is cruel. Why should he have been the exception? The rest of us learn it early. God is cruel, that is why we hate him and that is why we need him. We cannot comprehend the world otherwise. We do not deserve love, not in this life anyway. To tolerate the pain, that is our aspiration. That is all there is.

Henry   Jealousy!

Lucy   No, anger! Jealousy is God's prerogative. I am angry that he should have mistook his wife for the world – her love, for God's love. How dare he? With *his* mind! He set the trap for himself, and now she's dead. There is nowhere left for him to hide.

Henry   If God is as you paint him I think after all I prefer Galileo.

Lucy   I'm sure you do. The new science excludes sin, so naturally it is popular. But think, on your deathbed, when you are alone and despairing for breath, your veins burning and death staring you in the eye – then, Henry, will it be Galileo you call for? Will it be even your wife, who cannot follow where you go? Think on it, Henry, and tell me truly if God has gone, and that He is not cruel.

Henry   You are much changed.

Lucy   I am fortunate. I have stopped pretending.

Henry   He is desperate, Lucy. See him. He cannot endure without Ann.

Lucy   Then my presence will not help. Let his children tend him. Besides, there is virtue in desperation – he will learn much.

Henry   Religion has made you uncharitable.

Lucy   No, it has made me honest. We are too old for games, and there is not the time.

Henry   And what of friendship? Have we outgrown that, too?

Lucy (*erupts*)   I am tired of this cross-examination. This is neither a courtroom nor the court, it is my house! I begin to wonder for whom you are pleading. Do *you* miss me, Henry? Is that it? Do you still, somewhere, cultivate hope? Abandon it, Lord Wotton. I have but one husband, and beyond him I am wed to Jesus. In this Dr Donne and I are similar, I grant you that. We both see the only path of substance. Poor Henry. How alone you are. Go back to Venice, my Lord, to your intrigue and your masquing and the warm summer nights. England is too cold for you now.

Henry   You're right, Lucy. I do miss you.

Lucy   Goodbye, Lord Wotton.

Henry   Goodbye, my Lady Bedford.

Abruptly **Lucy** *turns and marches out.* **Esther** *enters tactfully.*

Henry   You are here to escort me to the door?

Esther (*curtseying*)   My Lord Wotton.

Henry   Your mistress is a remarkable woman, girl. You are fortunate to be in her employ.

Esther   Yes, sir.

Henry   But of course you know that. What else do you know, I wonder?

Esther   I do not know, sir.

Henry   And I thought myself the diplomat. Well, show me out.

Scene Eight

John *is revealed in his customary place by the side, writing at a table, but bodily discomforted and prematurely aged.* **Lucy** *enters. So does* **Ann***, unobtrusively; she listens throughout.*

Lucy   May I enter, Dr Donne?

He gestures; she does. She walks to the table. He does not rise. She picks up a page and reads to herself.

The Song? Was Layfield's translation not to your taste?

John   Layfield is dead.

Lucy   Yes. A great loss.

John (*toying with the phrase*)   A great loss.

Lucy   And you rewrite his work?

John   The work continues though the workers perish. Someone will rewrite me, one day.

Lucy   So you translate the translators. Very neat.

John   It would be, were it possible ever to finish the task.

Lucy   Oh?

John   Words move. Meanings are nudged sideways a little by every death and every birth. New ears, new tongues, forgotten senses. We die, the words continue – but differently, like ghostly messengers.

Lucy   Why bother? Who tallies the changes?

John   I don't know. Maybe God. Why have you come?

Lucy   I heard you were unwell.

John   As you see.

Lucy   You have my sympathy.

John   Oh, it will not kill me yet. I am in this world like a porter in a great house, ever nearest the door but seldomest abroad. Would I had leave to go.

Lucy   Desiring death is a sin, John. I'd have thought you would know that.

John   Is it? Why?

Lucy   It is for God to choose the manner of our dying. We are all in His hands.

John   Do you not see? Death has me already. I await only release. I long so to let go of this business of being someone.

Do you think those we bury are the dead? My poor girl.
Death happens to the living. The rest are past caring.

Lucy   They are tended elsewhere.

John   The child died too. The fifth.

Lucy   She is with God.

John   She is not with me!

Lucy   Are you so selfish?

John   Selfish? That's one of your puritan words. I do not
understand it.

Pause.

Ann was my self. She made me. I am self-less, without her.
She gave me form; alone I am smoke, dispersing far too
slowly in the spring breeze. I am an emptiness. Nothing left
to hold, now I can no longer hold her.

Lucy   Not so. You are at the service of your church.

John   As the bell serves the hour, and as hollow.

Lucy   You do your congregation ill, John.

John   No. A passing bell is enough for us all. They listen to
me and they hear the echo of their own dying. They are my
daily witnesses. I have the most wakeful church in London.

Lucy   So we both have stopped dreaming.

Reads further.

> 'Daughters of Jerusalem, swear to me
> That you will never awaken love
> Until it is ripe.'

John, did we love?

John (*with his former wit*)   I am for ever your Ladyship's
most absolute servant.

Lucy   Yes. That's what I thought. You will be well?

John   It is not my time, Lucy. And I have my daughters to care for me.

Lucy   Good. Farewell, John.

John   Goodbye Lucy.

She exits. **John** *searches through his papers. As he reads the following, he breaks down.*

Ann   'I am a wall
And my breasts are towers.
But for my lover I am
A city of peace.'

She holds him.

Slowly he recovers a little and stands, some of the pain leaving his body. He turns to the audience and delivers, as a much older man, a sermon from 1628. He begins in tears, but strengthens as he goes on.

Epilogue

John   So then this death is a sleep, and it delivers us to a present wakefulness. Those that sleep in Jesus, says the apostle, shall awake and declare that they have been in his hands since they departed this world. They shall awake as Jacob did, and say as Jacob said; surely the Lord is in this place, and this is no other but the house of God, and the gate of heaven. And into that gate they shall enter, and in that house they shall dwell, where there shall be no cloud nor sun, no darkness nor dazzling, but one equal light; no noise nor silence, but one equal music; no fears nor hopes, but one equal possession; no foes nor friends, but an equal communion and identity; no ends nor beginnings, but one equal eternity. Keep us Lord so awake in the duties of our calling that we may thus sleep in thy peace, and wake in thy glory, and change that infallibility which thou affordest us here, to an actual and undeterminable possession of that kingdom which thy Son, our Saviour Christ Jesus, hath purchased for us with the inestimable price of his incorruptible blood. Amen.

Ann *has been watching. Silently she approaches* **John** *once again and embraces him. They hold each other as the stage fades to black.*